R. Borland

Yarrow

Its Poets and Poetry

R. Borland

Yarrow
Its Poets and Poetry

ISBN/EAN: 9783337777685

Printed in Europe, USA, Canada, Australia, Japan

Cover: Foto ©Thomas Meinert / pixelio.de

More available books at **www.hansebooks.com**

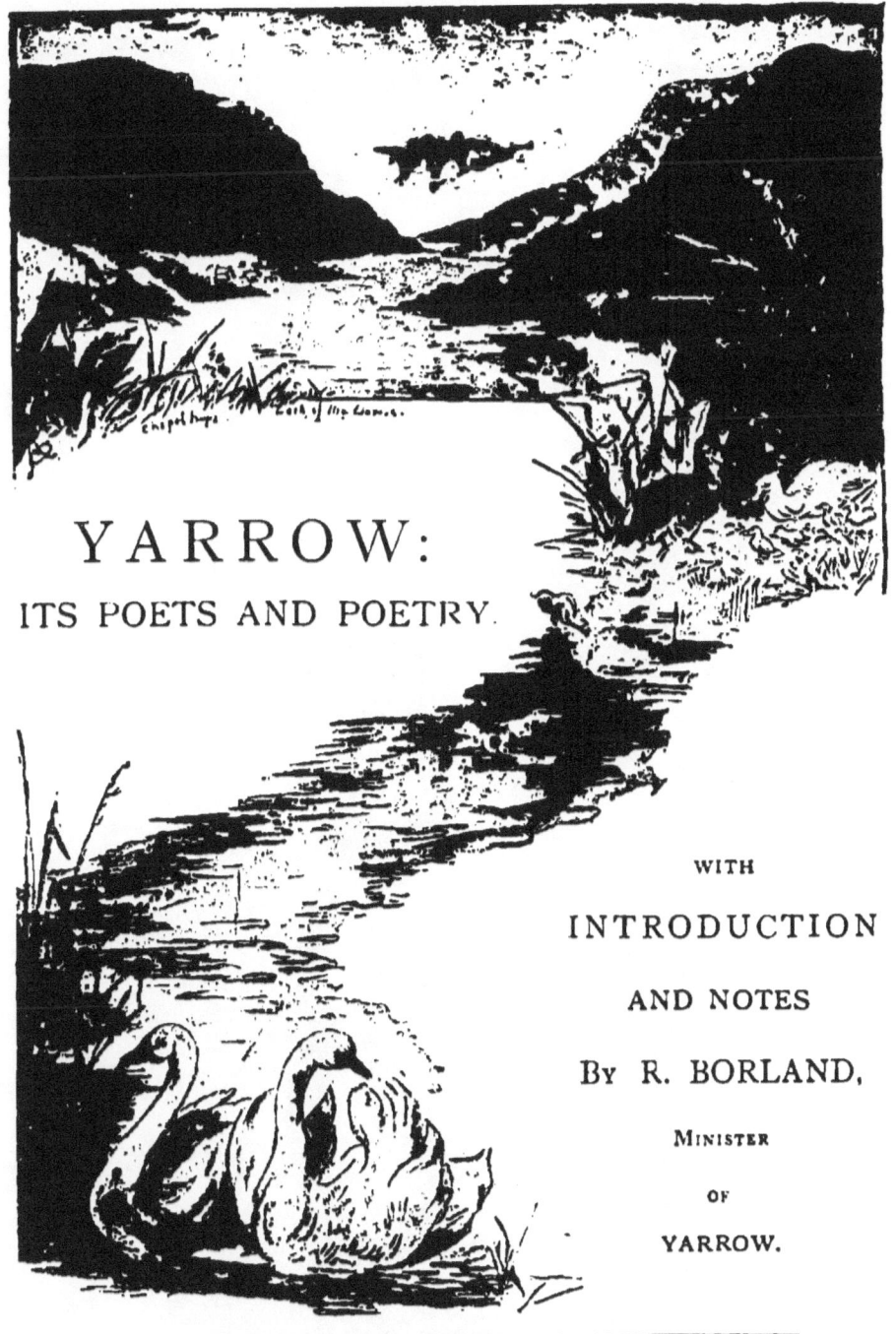

YARROW:
ITS POETS AND POETRY.

WITH

INTRODUCTION

AND NOTES

BY R. BORLAND,

MINISTER

OF

YARROW.

DALBEATTIE: THOMAS FRASER.
1890.

PREFACE.

THE object I have had in view in preparing this work
for the press has been to bring together the more
notable and interesting ballads and poems which Yarrow
has] inspired, and to give such brief biographical sketches of
the various poets as may prove either interesting or instructive
to the general reader. The task of making a judicious
selection from the mass of material which lay ready to hand
was none of the easiest, as Yarrow, for many generations,
has been a favourite theme of the votaries of the Muse. The
poems here published may be regarded as fairly representative
of the poetical literature of the valley. Many of them have
attained an almost world-wide celebrity; others of them,
perhaps, derive their chief interest from local or historical
associations, and a number of them are now printed for the
first time.

I have endeavoured to give the various ballads and poems,
as nearly as possible, in the form in which I have found
them, either in the works of their respective authors, or as
printed in the newspapers and magazines in which they
were originally published. This accounts for a certain variety
of spelling which the eager eye of the critic will be sure to
detect. In not a few cases the form of a poem, or ballad, has
become so familiar to the reader that to alter it, however

justifiable the change from a merely literary point of view, would create a feeling of disappointment. As far as possible, therefore, I have studiously refrained from interfering with the original text.

I have to express my heartiest thanks to all who have favoured me with contributions, and especially to my friends, Alex. Anderson and " J. B. Selkirk," for helpful suggestions in preparing the work for the press; also to Mr M. M'L. Harper, Castle-Douglas, and Mr Thos. Fraser, Dalbeattie, for their valuable assistance in correcting the proofs. I have to acknowledge the kindness of Macmillan & Co. for permission to use Principal Shairp's poem, "Three Friends in Yarrow," originally published in *Glen Desseray*. My warmest thanks are also due to Mrs Mangin for her sketches of Yarrow here reproduced.

The portion of the work for which I am more immediately responsible can lay no claim to any special literary merit. I have been mainly anxious to furnish whatever information may be necessary for the due appreciation of the local and historical setting of the various poems here brought together.

R. B.

MANSE OF YARROW,
    July 30th, 1890.

CONTENTS.

INTRODUCTION.

" Flow on for ever, Yarrow stream !
   Fulfil thy pensive duty,
  Well pleased that future bards should chant
  For simple hearts thy beauty."—WORDSWORTH.

THERE are few streams in any land that have been so
much besung as "ballad-haunted Yarrow." For
some hundreds of years it has had for the poetic mind a
strange, weird, almost irresistible fascination. Men of the
most diverse genius have come under its spell, and have
sung its praises in numbers characterised alike by strength
and tenderness of passion. And what is, perhaps, still more
remarkable—though Yarrow has many singers, the key-note of
all their songs is the same. There is a strain of sadness in the
music, an under-current of sorrow, giving a definite tone and
feeling to the whole. It seems impossible for any one who has
been touched by the spirit of the Vale to shake himself
altogether free from this feeling. Let the theme of his song be
what it may, let him sing with an air as jocund as the gayest
heart could wish, yet while we are listening to his inspiring
strains, we are conscious, as it were, that some one is playing a
dirge in the next room. "Somehow in the poetry of Yarrow,"
says Professor Veitch, "be it Ballad or Song, there is a deeper

B

tinge of sorrow (as compared with the Tweed), often a very
dark colouring, an almost overpowering sadness. The emotion
is that so finely expressed in a late period in ' The Flowers of
the Forest.' The feeling is as of a brief, bright morning, full
of promise, making the hills splendid and the heart glad, but ere
noon we have cloud and rain and tears, and evening closes
around us with only the memory of the vanished joy." Why
the prevailing tone of the literature of Yarrow should be so
uniformly one of sadness, it may be somewhat difficult satis-
factorily to explain. Professor Veitch, in his admirable work
on *The History and Poetry of the Scottish Border*, seems
of opinion that the configuration and general physical char-
acteristics of the district have had much to do in creating this
feeling of sadness. He says:—Nor will any one who is
familiar with the Vale of Yarrow have had much difficulty in
understanding how it is suited to pathetic verse. The rough
and broken, yet clear, beautiful and wide-spreading stream has
no grand cliffs to show; and it is not surrounded by high
and overshadowing hills. Here and there it flows placidly,
reflectively, in large liquid lapses, through an open valley of
the deepest summer green; still, let us be thankful, in its upper
reaches at least, mantled by nature and untouched by plough
or harrow. There is a placid monotone about its bare treeless
scenery—an unbroken pastoral stillness on the sloping braes
and hillsides, as they rise, fall, and bend in a uniformly
deep colouring. The silence of the place is forced upon the
attention, deepened even by the occasional break in the flow

of the stream, or by the bleating of the sheep that, white and motionless amid the pasture, dot the knowes. We are attracted by the silence, and we are also depressed. There is the pleasure of hushed enjoyment. The spirit of the scene is in these immortal lines :—

> ' Meek loveliness around thee spread,
> A softness still and holy ;
> The grace of forest charms decayed,
> And pastoral melancholy.'

Those deep green grassy knowes of the valley are peculiarly susceptible of change—of light and shade. In the morning with a blue sky, or with breaks of sunlight through the fleeting clouds, the green hillsides and the stream smile and gleam in sympathy with the cheerfulness of heaven.

"But under a grey sky, or at the gloamin', the Yarrow wears a peculiarly wan aspect—a look of sadness. And no valley I know is more susceptible of sudden change. The spirit of the air can speedily weave out of the mists that gather up on the massive hills at the heads of the Meggat and the Talla, a wide-spreading web of greyish cloud—the 'skaum' of the sky—that casts a gloom over the under green of the hills, and dims the face of loch and stream in a pensive shadow. The saddened heart would readily find there fit analogue and nourishment for its sorrow."

This description is perfect; but may not the same things be said of the Tweed, the Ettrick, and the Teviot; indeed of all the streams in the Border country? They have each an individuality of their own, but their general characteristics are the same.

And long ago when the whole country was covered with wood the resemblance must have been even more striking than it is now. Yarrow, especially in its upper reaches, is peculiarly bare, but in olden times it was well wooded, and must have presented an aspect as cheerful as any part of the surrounding country. Why its "houms" should be more "dowie" than those of the Tweed and Ettrick cannot be satisfactorily accounted for by the mere grouping of the physical peculiarities. These are neither in themselves so striking, nor unique, as to call for any special characterisation. The most pronounced features of the vale are common to all the tributaries of the Tweed.

Yet Yarrow has a history of her own. Her spirit is not that of her sister streams. She sings not less sweetly than they do, but there is a strange wail running through the music—a low murmur as of some one in pain. How is this to be accounted for? The most satisfactory explanation is, that "the red strain in the stream"—the cause of all the dool and sorrow—is due to the blood of those who have fallen in mortal combat. Such incidents as those which are commemorated in "The Dowie Dens" and "The Douglas Tragedy" must have produced a deep impression on the minds of the people, and though they were well accustomed to doughty deeds, yet such a rare combination of love and sorrow must have awakened the keenest and deepest feeling. But it may be said that these tragedies owe much of their power to the art of the poet. In dealing with such a theme, the poet does not concern himself about historical accuracy. His function—his primary function —is to excite feeling. In these incidents he found a theme which he could easily adapt to his purpose. The dauntless courage of the hero in "The Dowie Dens" is exceeded by the nnconquerable love of the heroine.

> "She kissed his cheek, she kaim'd his hair.
>   She searched his wounds all thorough;
> She kissed him till her lips grew red,
>   In the dowie houms of Yarrow."

Such ballads were destined to live in the memory and imagination of the people. They became an important factor in their daily life. The feeling they inspired was reflected on the scenes by which they were surrounded. The prevailing tone of "The Dowie Dens" has affected the whole subsequent literature of the district. We know that this ballad formed the groundwork of Hamilton of Bangour's exquisite lyric—"Busk ye, busk ye, my bonny, bonny bride"—and this in turn fascinated Wordsworth, whose three poems on Yarrow occupy an unique place among the many songs this stream has inspired.

The significant and highly important question as to the "secret" of Yarrow has been discussed in an able article from the pen of J. B. Selkirk, contributed to *Blackwood* in the year 1886. In discussing this question he says:—"The peculiar power exercised by Yarrow on her votaries is very significant. The result is not only the highest of its kind, but the whole product is fermented and characterised by a uniform local colour of pathetic passion which invests everything that has issued from that mint with a distinctive and unique individualism. The historical ballad, with one exception, that of 'The Outlaw Murray,' finds no place in Yarrow. 'The Dowie Dens,' 'The Lament of the Border Widow,' 'The Douglas Tragedy,' 'Willie's Drowned in Yarrow,' and many others, grow out of the social conditions and accidents of the times, and appeal to the ordinary emotions and instincts of humanity, and these have given the initial pathetic melancholy to everything that has followed . . . . These old pathetic singers have passed away and left no sign. They have crossed the river of death, and taken their secret with them. Unnamed and unknown as they are, they have, however, left behind them a magnetic witchery of vague and pathetic regret that cannot be shaken off or separated from the scene of their inspiration. No man of average sensibility ever entered that valley alone without coming to some extent under the weird fascination and endemic glamour of the place. Under its mysterious influence poets have been made and moulded like clay out of a cast." It would thus seem that the dominant and dominating influence is that exercised by the early literature of the valley. The "pastoral melancholy" which impressed Wordsworth so much has had but a small share in producing that element of "pathetic passion" which permeates the literature of Yarrow. The mind contemplates the scenery through the haze of local tradition, and the feeling produced is largely a result of the action of the subtle law of association After all it is not so much what the eye sees, as what it brings with it to the seeing; and in this case what is brought adds immensely to the effect. No species of literature, indeed, has ever more thoroughly taken possession of the imagination than the Yarrow ballads. It is impossible for any one who has ever read them to shake himself free from their weird fascination. The pictures are so perfectly drawn—the tragic element is so intense—the contrasts,—the deathless hate and unconquerable love, the blood-hound ferocity and angelic tenderness,—so strikingly represented—that there is produced on the mind an impression which neither lapse of time nor change of circumstance can possibly erase. Such tragedies never fail in investing a locality with a distinctive character; and in the present case it may be said that not *Nature*, but *human nature*, has made the "dens" of Yarrow "dowie."

Of the general characteristics of the ballads of Yarrow not much need be said here, as these are indicated in the notes. Suffice it to say that "The Song of the Outlaw Murray" is the only one of a distinctively historical cast: the others are essentially romantic. Few of them have been preserved in the form in which they were originally composed. In some of them, belonging without doubt to a remote period, we find words and phrases introduced which have a comparatively modern origin. Why this should be so is not difficult to explain. For many generations these ballads were dependant for their transmission upon the uncertain medium of oral tradition, and naturally enough the reciters, when they found that certain words or phrases had become obsolete, replaced them by others of a modern character, in order that they might make themselves sufficiently intelligible. Sometimes the critic, overlooking this fact, has been disposed to dispute the antiquity of certain ballads, because he happened to discover a word, or a phrase, that had an unmistakably modern origin. But the existence of such elements in no way invalidates an otherwise well-established claim to antiquity. "The desire of the reciter to be intelligible has been one of the greatest causes of the deterioration of the ballad. He discarded words that had become obsolete, and substituted for them expressions taken from the customs of his own day." "In general, however, the later reciters," says Sir Walter Scott, "appear to have been far less desirous to speak the author's words, than to introduce amendments and new readings of their own, which have always produced the effect of modernizing, and usually that of vulgarizing, the rugged sense and spirit of the antique minstrel. Thus, undergoing from age to age a gradual process of alteration and recomposition, our popular and oral minstrelsy has lost in a great measure its original appearance; and the strong touches by which it was originally characterised have been generally smoothed down and destroyed by a process similar to that by which a coin, passing from hand to hand, loses in circulation all the finer marks of the impress."

The Yarrow ballads have been subjected to the same influences. Not only has the phraseology been changed; but it has happened in some instances that stray verses from other ballads have become incorporated in a composition with which they have little or no affinity.

On the literary style of these ballads it is unnecessary to remark. The ancient bard was generally satisfied with a rude and careless form of expression, the very simplicity of the ballad stanza carrying with it a strong temptation to loose and trivial composition. But these ballads possess a deep interest for the student of literature, not only on account of the deeds they commemorate, but more especially on the ground that they afford a glimpse of the "national music in its cradle." We see here the first attempts at the formation of those tuneful sounds with which she was afterwards to charm posterity. They form a distinct and separate phase of literary history and achievement.

The poetical literature of Yarrow, subsequent to the ballad period, is at once varied in quality and extensive in quantity. Allan Ramsay was the first to take up the strain of the ancient minstrels, and his well-known songs "The Rose of Yarrow" and "Mary Scott" are pervaded by a tender feeling which, in some passages, swells into pathos. At the same time it may be justly remarked that his songs are more indebted to the theme for the interest they possess, than to any poetical qualities they display. Hogg was not far wrong when he said :

> " Redoubted Ramsay's peasant skill,
> Flung some strained notes along the hill;
> His was some lyre from lady's hall,
> And not the mountain harp at all."

The first poet who was destined to embalm the romance of Yarrow in imperishable verse was Hamilton of Bangour. His name and his fame as a poet will ever be associated with his

exquisite lyric—"The Braes of Yarrow." His other poems and
songs have well nigh passed into oblivion; but as long as
Yarrow has charms for the poetic mind this poem will never
fail in captivating the imagination. The stanzas are not all of
equal merit, but take it as a whole there are few finer things in
the poetical literature of the country. The wail of the old
·ballads resounds through its rhythmic cadences, like the low
weird "sough" of the wind among the autumn leaves of the
forest. The witching spell of this song has been thrown over
the whole subsequent literature of Yarrow, as the cloud, red-
tinged by the rays of the setting sun, casts a purple hue upon the
myriad streams that glint and gleam as they roll onward to the
sea. Wordsworth, Scott, Hogg, and many others, have felt
the power of its entrancing and bewitching strain, and had
Hamilton written nothing else he would still have been entitled
to a place among the immortals. If Spenser may be designated
"the poet's poet," Hamilton's "Braes of Yarrow" may be
regarded as the mystic font in which many a Yarrow minstrel
has received the baptism of the Muses.

It is unnecessary to enter fully into the merits of the many
songs which, within comparatively recent times, have garlanded
the braes of Yarrow with wreaths of immortal melody. Suffice
it to say that though Yarrow has occasioned more songs than
almost any other stream in the world, her power to confer a kind
of plenary inspiration does not seem to be on the wane.
J. B. Selkirk and Professor Veitch, Alexander Anderson and
Principal Shairp, Andrew Lang and Professor Blackie are

among the more recent of her poets, and though they differ widely in the manner in which they sing of the love and sorrow so inalienably associated with the vale, yet the feeling produced in the mind is that they are members of the same choir, each singing the part for which he is best fitted, and every note adding to the perfection of the symphony. And though the river still flows on as sweetly and softly as of yore, we seem to hear in its liquid melody a note which owns no material origin,—a strain of imaginative feeling, pathetic and yet sublime, now mingles, and shall ever mingle, with the music of the stream.

THE DOWIE DENS OF YARROW.

———————◆———————

THIS beautiful and pathetic ballad has attained an almost world-wide popularity. It has inspired many of the finest songs of which Yarrow is the theme, and has done more to enshrine the vale with a halo of romance than all other influences combined. Had "The Dowie Dens" never been sung or written the literary history of Yarrow might have been as meagre as that of many an all but nameless river. From this fountain of poetic inspiration myriad streams have issued to charm the world with their pensive sweetness and ideal beauty. The poesy of ancient Greece is not more closely related to the poetry of Homer or of English verse to the inspiring strains of Chaucer, than the poetical literature of Yarrow to "The Dowie Dens." Hamilton of Bangour found in this ballad the ground work of his beautiful poem, "The Braes of Yarrow," a poem which had evidently touched a deep chord in Wordsworth's heart, and had much to do in exciting the keen interest he displayed in the poetical traditions of the valley. The incident of the ballad may be said to have given a distinctive character to the district. There is nothing about the hills and glens which stretch out and up from the banks of the river to awaken a feeling of sadness in the mind of the spectator. Indeed there are many places in Scotland to which the term " dowie " might be more fitly applied ; but all the associations—in large part due to this tragedy—are plaintive and melancholy. This, and similar tragedies, must have produced a deep and lasting impression on the popular mind, and made those gladsome hills and fairy glens wear a melancholy aspect. The prevailing strain of this ballad furnishes the key note to the whole poetical literature of the district. There is an undertone of sorrow running through it, like the all but inaudible murmur of some hidden stream.

The combat which is here so felicitously described was betwixt a Scott of Tushielaw, and his brother-in-law, a Scott of Thirlestane, in which the latter was mortally wounded. The dispute was about some lands which old Tushielaw conveyed, or intended to convey, to his daughter. Professor Aytoun, in his book on *The Ballads of Scotland* expresses the opinion that Sir Walter Scott in the version he has given in the minstrelsy has mixed up two ballads—"The Dowie Dens," and "Willie's Drowned in Yarrow." He says—"The second ballad is on a totally different subject, and of another class, but exquisitely simple and pathetic. The two ballads being in the same measure were naturally enough confounded by the reciters ; and it seems to have escaped the notice of Sir Walter

Scott that the distinguishing peculiarity of the other ballad is
the uniformity of the rhyme in every stanza, the word 'Yarrow'

being throughout repeated.   I therefore think that his fine introductory verse,—

> "Late at e'en drinking the wine,
> And ere they paid the lawing,
> They set a combat them between
> To fight it in the dawing,"—

cannot be genuine.   And he has further introduced a verse which evidently belongs to the other ballad :—

> "O gentle wind that bloweth south,
> From where my love repaireth,
> Convey a kiss from his dear mouth,
> And tell me how he fareth."

There is another point in connection with the note appended to this ballad in the *Minstrelsy*, to which attention may be called. Sir Walter says:—"In ploughing 'Annan's Treat,' a huge monumental stone with an inscription was discovered; but being rather scratched than engraved, and the lines being run through each other, it is only possible to read one or two Latin words.   It probably records the event of the combat.   The person slain was the male ancestor of the present Lord Napier.

"Tradition affirms that the hero of the song (be he who he may) was murdered by the brother, either of his wife or betrothed bride.   The alleged cause of malice was the lady's father having proposed to endow her with half of his property, upon her marriage with a warrior of such renown.   The name of the murderer is said to have been Annan, and the place of combat is still called Annan's Treat.   It is a low moor lying to the west of Yarrow Kirk.   Two tall unhewn masses of stone are erected, about eighty yards from each other, and the least child that can herd a cow will tell the passenger that there lie 'the two lords who were slain in single combat.'"

The place where this monumental stone was discovered is not known as Annan's Treat, but as Annan Street. The inscription on the stone bears that it was erected by *Liberalis* to the memory of his two sons. The following is the translation given by Dr Smith:—"Here Memor Lies of Loinrisnus (The Son) Princes (or Chieftains of) Cnudus (and) Dumnogenus. Here lie in the Tumulus, two sons of Liberalis." Professor Rhys, the well-known Celtic scholar, is of opinion that this interesting monumental slab dates back to the fifth or sixth century of our era, and by no stretch of the imagination can it be supposed to have had any connection with "The Tragedy of the Dowie Dens." There are really *four* stones standing about two hundred yards apart. The first is at the side of the Whitehope burn, a few yards from the entrance to the church; the second at the shepherd's house, called "The Warrior's Rest;" the third, which tradition has fixed upon as the scene of tragedy, in the glebe; the fourth—"the inscribed stone"—in a field on the farm of Whitehope. That a great battle had been fought in this neighbourhood is highly probable. The name given to the place, "Warrior's Rest," is in itself suggestive; but proof of a more convincing nature was forthcoming when the Rev. Dr. Robert Russell, the father of the late genial and gifted author of *Reminiscences of Yarrow*, enclosed the fields to the west of the church. On removing various heaps of stones he found considerable quantities of

c

bone dust, clearly enough indicating that here, in this primitive fashion, many bodies had been buried. Several stone cists, full of remains, have been discovered in this region, one of which has been exposed to observation near the shepherd's house.

The ballad of "The Dowie Dens" was first published in Scott's *Border Minstrelsy,* and though it bears evident traces of interpolation, it has, through this medium, become so well known, and is otherwise of such distinguished merit, that it is to be preferred to the more accurate, but less picturesque form of the ballad which Professor Aytoun has published in his *Ballads of Scotland.* Professor Veitch, a recognised authority on all subjects pertaining to the history and poetry of the Borders, justly remarks that "for brevity, directness, and graphic turn of narrative, vivid picturing, and the image of passionate devotion to the dead, there are few ballads in any language that match its strains."

> LATE at e'en, drinking the wine,
>   And ere they paid the lawing,
> They set a combat them between,
>   To fight it in the dawing.

> " O stay at hame, my noble lord !
>   O stay at hame, my marrow !
> My cruel brother will you betray,
>   On the dowie houms of Yarrow."—

" O fare ye weel, my ladye gaye !
  O fare ye weel, my Sarah !
For I maun gae, though I ne'er return
  Frae the dowie banks o' Yarrow."—

She kiss'd his cheek, she kaim'd his hair,
  As oft she had done before, O ;
She belted him with his noble brand,
  And he's away to Yarrow.

As he gaed up the Tennies bank,
  I wot he gaed wi' sorrow,
Till, down in a den, he spied nine arm'd men,
  On the dowie houms of Yarrow.

" O come ye here to part your land,
  The bonnie Forest thorough ?
Or come ye here to wield your brand,
  On the dowie houms of Yarrow ?"—

" I come not here to part my land,
  And neither to beg nor borrow ;
I come to wield my noble brand,
  On the bonnie banks of Yarrow."

If I see all, ye're nine to ane,
  And that's an unequal marrow,
Yet will I fight, while lasts my brand,
  On the bonnie banks o' Yarrow.

Four has he hurt, and five has slain,
   On the bloody braes of Yarrow,
Till that stubborn knight came him behind,
   And ran his body thorough.

" Gae hame, gae hame, good-brother John,
   And tell your sister Sarah,
To come and lift her leafu' lord ;
   He's sleepin' sound on Yarrow."—

Yestreen I dream'd a dolefu' dream ;
   I fear there will be sorrow !
I dream'd I pu'd the heather green,
   Wi' my true love on Yarrow.

" But in the glen strive armed men ;
   They've wrought me dole and sorrow ;
They've slain—the comliest knight they've slain—
   He bleeding lies on Yarrow.

As she sped down yon high high hill,
   She gaed wi' dole and sorrow,
And in the den spied ten slain men,
   On the dowie banks of Yarrow.

She kissed his cheek, she kaim'd his hair,
   She searched his wounds all thorough,
She kiss'd them till her lips grew red,
   On the dowie houms of Yarrow.

" Now haud your tongue, my daughter dear
  For a' this breeds but sorrow ;
I'll wed ye to a better lord,
  Than him ye lost on Yarrow."—

" O haud your tongue, my father dear !
  Ye mind me but of sorrow;
A fairer rose did never bloom
  Than now lies cropp'd on Yarrow."

WILLIE'S DROWNED IN YARROW.

THIS ballad from its touching sentiment and natural pathos has always been popular. It has frequently been printed with variations, but Professor Aytoun is of opinion that the version given by him in *The Ballads of Scotland* is genuine, and on the authority of that learned and conscientious compiler we have given it here.

" WILLIE'S rare and Willie's fair,
    And Willie's wondrous bonny,
And Willie's hecht to marry me,
    Gin e'er he married ony.

" Yestreen I made my bed fu' braid,
    This night I'll make it narrow,
For a' the live long winter night
    I'll lie twin'd of my marrow.

" O gentle wind that bloweth south,
    From where my love repaireth,
Convey a kiss from his dear mouth,
    And tell me how he fareth.

" O tell sweet Willie to come doun,
    And bid him no be cruel,
And tell him no to break the heart
    Of his love and only jewel.

" O tell sweet Willie to come doun,
    And hear the mavis singing ;
And see the birds on ilka bush,
    And leaves around them hinging.

" O cam' ye by yon water side ?
    Pu'd ye the rose or lily ?
Or cam' ye by yon meadow green ?
    Or saw ye my sweet Willie ?"

She sought him east, she sought him west,
    She sought him braid and narrow ;
Syne, in the cleaving of a craig,
    She fand him drown'd in Yarrow.

TAMLANE.

————◆————

THE scene of this ballad is laid at Carterhaugh, a plain at the confluence of the Yarrow and the Ettrick, two miles above Selkirk. The young Tamlane, who describes himself as a son of Randolph, Earl Murray, having been sent for when just turned nine, to keep his uncle company in hunting, hawking, and riding, was, while on his journey, thrown by a sharp north wind into a dead sleep, and fell from his horse, when the Queen of Fairies carried him off for herself. His experiences in fairyland, the reason why he wished to leave it, and the manner in which his rescue was to be effected, are all graphically described. The ballad is undoubtedly of great antiquity. It is referred to in *The Complaynt of Scotland*, a book which was printed at St. Andrews in 1549. The version given is from Aytoun's *Ballads of Scotland*.

" O I forbid ye, maidens a',
    That bind in snood your hair,
To come or gae by Carterhaugh,
    For young Tamlane is there."

Fair Janet sat within her bower,
    Sewing her silken seam,
And fain would be at Carterhaugh,
    Amang the leaves sae green.

She's prink'd hersell, and preen'd hersell,
   By the ae light o' the moon,
And she's awa to Carterhaugh,
   As fast as she could gang.

She hadna pu'd a red red rose,
   A rose but barely three,
When up and starts the young Tamlane,
   Says, " Lady, let a-be !

" What gars ye pu' the rose, Janet ?
   What gars ye break the tree ?
Or why come ye to Carterhaugh,
   Without the leave o' me ?"

" O I will pu' the flowers," she said,
   " And I will break the tree ;
For Carterhaugh it is my ain,
   I'll ask nae leave of thee."

He took her by the milk-white hand,
   And by the grass-green sleeve,
And laid her down upon the flowers,
   Nor ever asked her leave.

" Now ye maun tell the truth," she said,
   " A word ye maunna lie ;
O, were ye ever in haly chapel,
   Or sained in Christentie ?"

" The truth I'll tell to thee, Janet,
    A word I winna lie ;
 I was ta'en to the good church-door,
    And sained as well as thee.

" Randolph, Earl Murray, was my sire,
    Dunbar, Earl March, was thine ;
 We loved when we were children small,
    Which still you yet may mind.

" When I was a boy just turned of nine,
    My uncle sent for me,
 To hunt, and hawk, and ride with him,
    And keep him companie.

" There came a wind out of the north,
    A sharp wind and a snell,
 And a dead sleep came over me,
    And frae my horse I fell ;
 The Queen of Fairies she was there,
    And took me to hersell.

" And never would I tire, Janet,
    In fairy-land to dwell,
 But aye, at every seven years,
    They pay the teind to hell ;
 And I'm sae fat and fair of flesh,
    I fear 'twill be mysell !

" The morn at e'en is Hallowe'en,
        Our fairy court will ride,
    Through England and through Scotland baith,
        And through the warld sae wide,
    And if that ye wad borrow me,
        At Miles Cross ye maun bide.

" And ye maun gae to the Miles Moss,
        Between twelve hours and one,
    Tak' haly water in your hand,
        And cast a compass roun'."

" And how shall I ken thee, Tamlane ?
        And how shall I thee knaw,
    Amang the throng o' fairy folk,
        The like I never saw ?"

" The first court that comes along,
        Ye'll let them a' pass by ;
    The neist court that comes along
        Salute them reverently.

" The third court that comes along
        Is clad in robes o' green,
    And it's the head court of them a',
        And in it rides the Queen.

" And I upon a milk-white steed,
        Wi' a gold star in my crown ;
    Because I am a christened man,
        They give me that renown.

" Ye'll seize upon me with a spring,
    And to the ground I'll fa',
And then ye'll hear an elrish cry
    That Tamlane is awa'.

" They'll turn me in your arms, Janet,
    An adder and a snake ;
But haud me fast, let me not pass,
    Gin ye wad be my maik.

" They'll turn me in your arms, Janet,
    An adder and an aske,
They'll turn me in your arms, Janet,
    A bale that burns fast.

" They'll shape me in your arms, Janet,
    A dove, but and a swan,
And last they'll shape me in your arms
    A mother-naked man :
Cast your green mantle over me—
    And sae shall I be wan !"

Gloomy, gloomy was the night,
    And eerie was the way,
As fair Janet, in her green mantle,
    To Miles Cross she did gae.

There's haly water in her hand,
    She casts a compass round ;
And straight she sees a fairy band
    Come riding o'er the mound.

And first gaed by the black, black steed,
    And then gaed by the brown ;
But fast she gript the milk-white steed,
    And pu'd the rider down.

She pu'd him frae the milk-white steed,
    And loot the bridle fa' ;
And up their raise an elrish cry :
    " He's won amang us a' !"

They shaped him in fair Janet's arms,
    An aske, but and an adder;
She held him fast in every shape,
    To be her ain true lover.

They shaped him in her arms at last
    A mother-naked man,
She cuist her mantle over him,
    And sae her true love wan.

Up then spake the Queen o' Fairies,
    Out of a bush o' broom :
" She that has borrowed young Tamlane,
    Has gotten a stately groom !"

Up then spake the Queen o' Fairies
    Out of a bush of rye :
" She's ta'en away the bonniest knight
    In a' my companie !

" But had I kenned, Tamlane," she says,
  " A lady would borrow thee,
 I wad hae ta'en out thy twa grey e'en,
    Put in twa e'en o' tree !

" Had I but kenned, Tamlane," she says,
  " Before ye came frae hame,
 I wad hae ta'en out your heart of flesh,
    Put in a heart o' stane !

" Had I but had the wit yestreen
    That I hae coft this day,
 I'd hae paid my kane seven times to hell
    Ere you'd been won away !"

THE SONG OF THE OUTLAW MURRAY.

THIS interesting historical ballad was composed during the reign of James V. The tragic event which it commemorates took place betwixt a Scottish monarch and an ancestor of the family of Murray of Philiphaugh, in the county of Selkirk. It would seem that the Murrays, like other Border clans in that age, were in a lawless state. They had no proper title to their lands, but held them, like all the proprietors in Ettrick Forest, merely by occupancy. Such a condition of affairs was not favourable to the public peace. There was constant confusion and disturbance. The kings of Scotland were sometimes unable, owing to the weakness of their own position, to hold in check the more powerful and daring among their often rebellious subjects. The result was that they had not infrequently to compromise matters, and accept terms not fully in harmony with the assumed dignity of their position. James at one time was under the painful necessity of entering into a kind of league with Johnnie Faa, the King of the Gipsies.

There is therefore nothing improbable in the tradition which has been handed down in this song. The likelihood is that it had some considerable foundation in fact.

The popular opinion is that the scene of the ballad was Newark, an old Border stronghold, standing on the banks of the Yarrow, four miles above Selkirk. But as Sir Walter Scott has pointed out, this supposition is extremely improbable, as Newark was always a royal fortress. The seat of the Murray family for many generations was the Tower of Hangingshaw, a stronghold situated in a commanding position, two miles west from Newark, at the base of the Lewinshope Ridge. A finer situation for a fortress could hardly be conceived. In those days when the surrounding hills were covered with copse it must have been all but impregnable. The Hangingshaw estate has been for many years in the possession of the Johnstones of Alva, an old and well-known Scottish family. The old castle has entirely disappeared, not one stone being left to mark the place where it stood.

According to tradition, the Outlaw was a man of prodigious strength, and with his baton laid waste the country for miles around. How he met with his death is not accurately known. One tradition speaks of him as having been slain by Buccleuch, or one of his clan; another bears that he was shot by Scott of Haining near to the house of the Duke of Buccleuch's gamekeeper, beneath the Castle of Newark.

> ETTRICKE Foreste is a feir foreste,
>   In it grows manie a semelie tree;
> There's hart and hynd, and dae and rae,
>   And of a' wild bestis grete plentie.

There's a feir castelle, bigged wi' lime and stane,
   O! gin it stands not pleasauntlie!
In the fore front o' that castelle feir,
   Twa unicorns are bra' to see;
There's the picture of a knight, and a ladye bright,
   And the grene hollin abune their brie.

There an Outlaw kepis five hundred men;
   He keepis a royalle cumpanie!
His merryemen are a' in ae liverye clad,
   O' the Lincome grene sae gaye to see;
He and his ladye in purple clad,
   O! gin they lived not royallie!

Word is gane to our nobil King,
   In Edinburgh where that he lay,
That there was an Outlaw in Ettricke Foreste
   Counted him nought, nor a' his courtrie gay.

"I make a vowe," then the gude King said,
   "Unto the man that deir bought me,
I'se either be King of Ettricke Foreste,
   Or King of Scotlande that Outlaw sall be!"

Then spake the lord hight Hamilton,
   And to the nobil King said he,
"My sovereign prince, some counsell take,
   First at your nobilis, syne at me.

" I redd ye, send yon braw Outlaw till,
    And see gif your man cum will he :
Desyre him cum and be your man,
    And hold of you, yon Foreste frie.

" Gif he refuses to do that,
    We'll conquess baith his landis and he !
Or else, we'll throw his castelle down,
    And make a widow o' his gaye ladye."—

The King then call'd a gentleman,
    James Boyd (the Earle of Arran his brother was he;)
When James he cam before the King,
    He knelit before him on his kné.

" Wellcum, James Boyd !" said our nobil King,
    " A message ye maun gang for me ;
Ye maun hye to Ettricke Foreste
    To yon Outlaw, where bydeth he :

" Ask him of whom he haldis his landis,
    Or man, wha may his master be,
And desyre him cum, and be my man,
    And hold of me yon Foreste frie.

" To Edinburgh to cum and gang,
    His safe warrant I sall gie ;
And gif he refuses to do that,
    We'll conquess baith his landis and he.

D2

" Thou mayst vow I'll cast his castell down,
    And mak a widowe o' his gaye ladye ;
I'll hang his merryemen, payr by payr,
    In ony frith where I may them see."—

James Boyd tuik his leave o' the nobil King,
    To Ettricke Foreste feir cam he ;
Down Birkendale Brae when that he cam,
    He saw the feir Foreste wi' his ee.

Baith dae and rae, and harte and hinde,
    And of a' wild bestis great plentie ;
He heard the blows that bauldly ring,
    And arrows whidderan' hym near bi.

Of that feir castell he got a sight ;
    The like he neir saw wi' his ee !
On the fore front of that castell feir,
    Twa unicorns were gaye to see ;
The picture of a knight, and ladye bright,
    And the grene hollin abune their brie.

Thereat he spyed five hundred men,
    Shuting with bows on Newark Lee ;
They were a' in ae livery clad,
O' the Lincome grene sae gaye to see.

His men were a' clad in the grene,
    The knight was armed capapie,
With a bended bow, on a milk-white steed ;
    And I wot they rank'd right bonnilie.

Thereby Boyd kend he was master man,
　　And served him in his ain degré
" God mot thee save, brave Outlaw Murray !
　　Thy ladye, and all thy chyvalrie !"—
" Marry, thou's wellcum, gentlemen,
　　Some king's messenger thou seemis to be."—

" The King of Scotlonde sent me here,
　　And, gude Outlaw, I am sent to thee ;
I wad wot of whom ye hald your landis,
　　O man, who may thy master be ?"—

" Thir landis are MINE !" the Outlaw said ;
　　" I ken nae King in Christentie ;
Frae Soudron I this Foreste wan,
　　When the King nor his knightis were not to see."—

" He desyres you'l cum to Edinburgh,
　　And hauld of him this Foreste fre ;
And, gif ye refuse to do this,
　　He'll conquess baith thy landis and thee.
He hath vow'd to cast thy castell down,
　　And mak' a widowe o' thy gaye ladye."

" He'll hang thy merryemen, payr by payr,
　　In ony frith where he may them finde."—
" Ay, by my troth !" the Outlaw said,
　　" Than wauld I think me far behinde.

"Ere the King my feir countrie get,
    This land that's nativest to me!
Mony o' his nobilis sall be cauld,
    Their ladyes sall be right wearie."—

Then spak his ladye, feir of face,
    She seyd, "Without consent of me,
That an Outlaw suld cum before a king;
    I am right rad of treasonrie.
Bid him be gude to his lordis at hame,
    For Edinburgh my lord sall nevir see."—

James Boyd tuik his leave o' the Outlaw kene,
    To Edinburgh boun is he;
When James he cam before the King,
    He knelit lowlie on his kné.

"Welcum, James Boyd!" seyd our nobil King;
    "What foreste is Ettricke Foreste frie?"—
"Ettricke Foreste is the feirest foreste
    That evir man saw wi' his ee.

"There's the dae, the rae, the hart, the hynde,
    And of a' wild bestis grete plentie;
There's a pretty castell of lyme and stane,
    O! gif it standis not pleasauntlie!

"There's in the fore front o' that castell,
    Twa unicorns, sae bra' to see,
There's the picture of a knight, and a ladye bright,
    Wi' the grene hollin abune their brie.

THE SONG OF THE OUTLAW MURRAY.

" There the Outlaw keepis five hundred men,
    He keepis a royalle companie !
His merryemen in ae livery clad,
    O' the Lincome grene sae gaye to see :
He and his ladye in purple clad ;
    O ! gin they live not royallie !

" He says yon Foreste is his awin ;
    He wan it frae the Southronie ;
Sae as he wan it, sae will he keep it,
    Contrair all kingis in Christentie !—

" Gar warn me Perthshire, and Angus baith ;
    Fife up and downe, and Louthians three,
And graith my horse !" said our nobil King,
    " For to Ettricke Foreste hie will I me."—

Then word is gane the Outlaw till,
    In Ettricke Foreste, where dwelleth he,
That the King was cuming to his cuntrie,
    To conquess baith his landis and he.

" I mak a vow," the Outlaw said,
    " I mak a vow, and that trulie,
Were there but three men to tak my pairt,
    Your King's cuming full deir suld be !"—

Then messengers he called forth,
    And bade them hie them speedilye—
" Ane of ye gae to Halliday,
    The Laird of the Corehead is he."

" He certain is my sister's son ;
 Bid him cum quick and succour me !
The King cums on for Ettricke Foreste,
 And landless men we a' will be."—

" What news ? What news ?" said Halliday ;
 " Man, frae thy master unto me ?"—
" Not as ye wad ; seeking your aíde ;
 The King's his mortal enemie."—

" Ay, by my troth !" said Halliday,
 " Even for that it repenteth me ;
For gif he lose feir Ettricke Foreste,
 He'll tak feir Moffatdale frae me."

" I'll meet him wi' five hundred men,
 And surely mair, if mae may be ;
And before he gets the Foreste feir,
 We a' will die on Newark Lee !"—

The Outlaw call'd a messenger,
 And bid him hie him speedilye,
To Andrew Murray of Cockpoole—
 " That man's a deir cousin to me ;
Desyre him cum, and make me aide,
 With a' the power that he may be."—

" It stands me hard," Andrew Murray said,
 " Judge gif it stand na hard wi' me ;
To enter against a King wi' crown,
 And set my landis in jeopardie !
Yet, if I cum not on the day,
 Surely at night he sall me see."—

To Sir James Murray of Traquair,
　A message came right speedilye—
"What news ? What news ?" James Murray said,
　"Man, frae thy master unto me ?"—

"What neids I tell ? for weel ye ken
　The King's his mortal enemie ;
And now he is cuming to Ettricke Foreste,
　And landless men ye a' will be."—

"And, by my trothe," James Murray said,
　"Wi' that Outlaw will I live and die ;
The King has gifted my landis lang syne—
　It cannot be nae warse wi' me."

The King was cuming thro' Caddon Ford,
　And full five thousand men was he ;
They saw the derke Foreste them before,
　They thought it awsome for to see.

Then spak the Lord, hight Hamilton,
　And to the nobil King said he,
"My sovereign liege, sum council tak,
　First at your nobilis, syne at me.

"Desyre him mete thee at Permanscore
　And bring four in his cumpanie ;
Five Erles sall gang yoursell befor,
　Gude cause that you suld honour'd be.

" And, gif he refuses to do that,
    We'll conquess baith his landis and he ;
There sall nevir a Murray, after him,
    Hald land in Ettricke Foreste free."—

Then spak the kene Laird of Buckscleuth,
    A stalworthe man, and sterne was he—
" For a King to gang an Outlaw till,
    Is beneath his state and his dignitie.

" The man that wons yon Foreste intill,
    He lives by reif and felonie !
Wherefore, brayd on, my sovereign liege,
    Wi' fire and sword we'll follow thee ;
Or, gif your courtrie lords fa' back,
    Our Borderers sall the onset gie."—

Then out and spak the nobil King,
    And round him cast a wilie ee—
" Now, had thy tongue, Sir Walter Scott,
    Nor speak of reif nor felonie :
For, had every honest man his awin kye,
    A right puir clan thy name wad be !"—

The King then call'd a gentleman,
    Royal banner-bearer there was he ;
James Hoppringle, of Torsonse, by name ;
    He cam and knelit upon his kné.

" Wellcum, James Pringle of Torsonse !
  A message ye maun gang for me :
You maun gae to yon Outlaw Murray,
  Surely where bauldly bideth he.

" Bid him mete me at Permanscore,
  And bring four in his cumpanie ;
Five erles sall cum wi' mysel,
  Gude reason I suld honour'd be ;

" And gif he refuses to do that,
  Bid him luke for nae gude o' me !
There sall nevir a Murray, after him,
  Have land in Ettricke Foreste free."

James cam before the Outlaw kene,
  And served him in his ain degré,—
Wellcum, James Pringle of Torsonse !
  What message frae the King to me ?"—

" He bids ye meet him at Permanscore,
  And bring four in your cumpany,
Five erles sall gang himsell befor,
  Nae mair in number will he be.

" And gif you refuse to do that,
  (I freely here upgive wi' thee),
He'll cast yon bonny castle down,
  And make a widowe o' that gaye ladye.

" He'll loose yon bluidhound Borderers,
 Wi' fire and sword to follow thee ;
There will nevir a Murray, after thysell,
 Have land in Ettricke Foreste free."—

" It stands me hard," the Outlaw said ;
 " Judge gif it stands na hard wi' me,
Wha reck not losing of mysell,
 But a' my offspring after me.

" My merryemen's lives, my widowe's teirs—
 There lies the pang that pinches me ;
When I am straught in bludie eard,
 Yon castell will be right dreirie.

" Auld Halliday, young Halliday,
 Ye sall be twa to gang wi' me ;
Andrew Murray, and Sir James Murray,
 We'll be nae mae in cumpanie."—

When that they cam before the King,
 They fell before him on their kné—
" Grant mercie, mercie, nobil King !
 E'en for his sake that dyed on tree."—

" Sicken like mercie sall ye have ;
 On gallows ye sall hangit be !"—
" Over God's forbode," quoth the Outlaw then,
 I hope your grace will bettir be !
Else, ere ye come to Edinburgh port,
 I trow thin guarded sall ye be:

" Thir landis of Ettricke Foreste fair,
    I wan them from the enemie ;
Like as I wan them, sae will I keep them,
    Contrair a' kingis in Christentie."—

All the nobilis the King about,
    Said pitie it were to see him dee—
" Yet grant me mercie, sovereign prince,
    Extend your favour unto me !

" I'll give you the keys of my castell,
    Wi' the blessing o' my gaye ladye,
Gin thou'll make me sheriffe of this Foreste,
    And a' my offspring after me."—

" Will thou give me the keys of thy castell,
    Wi' the blessing o' thy gaye ladye ?
I'se make thee sheriffe of Ettricke Foreste,
    Surely while upward grows the tree ;
If you be not traitour to the king,
    Forfaulted sall thou nevir be."—

" But, Prince, what sall cum o' my men ?
    When I gae back, traitour they'll ca' me,
I had rather lose my life and land,
    Ere my merryemen rebuked me."—

"Will your merryemen amend their lives ?
    And a' their pardons I grant thee—
Now, name thy landis where'er they lie,
    And here I RENDER them to thee."—

" Fair Philiphaugh is mine by right,
    And Lewinshope still mine shall be ;
Newark, Foulshiells, and Tinnies baith,
    My bow and arrow purchased me.

" And I have native steads to me,
    The Newark Lee and Hangingshaw,
I have mony steads in the Foreste schaw,
    But them by name I dinna knaw."

The keys of the castell he gave the King,
    Wi' the blessing o' his feir ladye ;
He was made sheriffe of Ettricke Foreste,
    Surely while upward grows the tree ;
And if he was na traitour to the King.
    Forfaulted he suld never þe.

Wha ever heard, in ony times,
    Sicken an outlaw in his degré,
Sic favour get before a King,
    As did the OUTLAW MURRAY of the Foreste free ?

THE DOUGLAS TRAGEDY.

THE incident here recorded is of a similar nature to that of "The Dowie Dens." The scene of the tragedy is in the Glen of Blackhouse, a wild romantic region, through which flows the Douglas Burn joining the Yarrow below the public road in the neighbourhood of the Craig. "Blackhouse was a very old possession of the great house of Douglas. One of the family sat in a Parliament of Malcolm Canmore at Forfar, as baronial lord of Douglas Burn. Whether or not the lady who fled from her father's tower was a Douglas, it is now impossible to say. But if she were, this would account for the disparity in social rank between herself and her lover, at which tradition hints. The bridle-road across the hills, which the fleeing lovers are said to have followed, can still be easily traced. It is one of the main old Border roads or riding tracks between the Yarrow and the Tweed. From Blackhouse Tower, it leads along the broad hill tops by way of the Hundleshope, or by Crookstone, to the Tweed at Peebles, proceeding across the watershed of the Douglas, Glenrath and Glensax Burns, and by the ridge of the Fa' Seat—the highest of the hills in that wild district. From the central path various branches of roads diverge, each traceable still to some ancient peel, with which it afforded a ready connection to the mounted Borderer. The

knight and his lady love were making their way to the home of
the former when overtaken by her father and her seven brothers.
The stones which are said to mark the scene of the fatal conflict
are, however, greatly older than any reasonable date which can
be assigned to the story of the ballad, and, instead of their being
only seven, as is commonly alleged, there are eleven in all now
visible.   Three of these are still standing, and eight are lying
flat on the ground.   In form they present the appearance of a
semi-circle, the section forming the base lying to the north or
up the hill.   The breadth of the section at the base is fifteen
paces, or about forty-five feet.   The distance of every stone ·in
the circle from its neighbour seems to have been nine paces, or
twenty seven feet.   The structure obviously belongs to the
general class of stone circles common on the Lowland hills,
which might have been places of judicature, or worship, or
burial, or all three.   Still it is quite possible that in this, as in
other instances, these ancient stones became the scene of a
historical event." (*History and Poetry of Scottish Border*,
pp. 407-8.)

" RISE up, rise up, now, Lord Douglas," she says,
   " And put on your armour so bright;
   Let it never be said that a daughter of thine
      Was married to a lord under night.

" Rise up, rise up, my seven bold sons,
      And put on your armour so bright,
   And take better care of your youngest sister,
      For your eldest's awa' the last night."—

He's mounted her on a milk-white steed,
    And himself on a dapple grey,
With a bugelet horn hung down by his side,
    And lightly they rode away.

Lord William lookit o'er his left shoulder,
    To see what he could see,
And there he spy'd her seven brethren bold,
    Come riding o'er the lee.

" Light down, light down, Lady Marg'ret," he said,
    " And hold my steed in your hand,
Until that against your seven brethren bold,
    And your father, I make a stand."—

She held his steed in her milk-white hand,
    And never shed one tear,
Until that she saw her seven brethren fa',
    And her father hard fighting, who loved her so dear.

" O hold your hand, Lord William !" she said,
    " For your strokes they are wondrous sair ;
True lovers I can get many a ane,
    But a father I can never get mair."—

O she's ta'en out her handkerchief,
    It was o' the holland sae fine,
And aye she dighted her father's bloody wounds,
    That were redder than the wine.

E

"O chuse, O chuse, Lady Marg'ret," he said,
  "O whether will ye gang or bide?"—
"I'll gang, I'll gang, Lord William," she said,
  "For you have left me no other guide."—

He's lifted her on a milk-white steed,
  And himself on a dapple grey,
With a bugelet horn hung down by his side,
  And slowly they baith rade away.

O they rade on, and on they rade,
  And a' by the light of the moon,
Until they came to yon wan water,
  And there they lighted down.

They lighted down to tak a drink
  Of the spring that ran sae clear;
And down the stream ran his gude heart's blood,
  And sair she 'gan to fear.

"Hold up, hold up, Lord William," she says,
  "For I fear that you are slain!"—
"'Tis naething but the shadow of my scarlet cloak,
  That shines in the water sae plain."—

O they rade on, and on they rade,
  And a' by the light of the moon,
Until they cam to his mother's ha' door,
  And there they lighted down.

" Get up, get up, lady mother," he says,
   " Get up, and let me in !—
Get up, get up, lady mother," he says,
   " For this night my fair lady I've win.

" O mak my bed, lady mother," he says,
   " O mak it braid and deep !
And lay Lady Marg'ret close at my back,
   And the sounder I will sleep."—

Lord William was dead lang ere midnight,
   Lady Marg'ret lang ere day—
And all true lovers that go thegither,
   May they have mair luck than they !

Lord William was buried in St. Marie's Kirk,
   Lady Marg'ret in Marie's quire ;
Out o' the lady's grave grew a bonny red rose,
   And out o' the knight's a brier.

And they twa met, and they twa plat,
   And fain they wad be near;
And a' the warld might ken right weel,
   They were twa lovers dear.

But bye and rade the Black Douglas,
   And wow but he was rough !
For he pull'd up the bonny brier,
   And flang'd in St. Marie's Loch.

THE BORDER WIDOW'S LAMENT.

———————◆———————

THE following is in some respects one of the most interesting of all the Border ballads. It is suffused by a pathetic feeling as tender and touching as anything of the kind ever produced. The scene is vividly portrayed: every detail of the sad story stamps itself indelibly upon the memory, and captivates the imagination with an irresistible fascination. The disconsolate widow weeping over her murdered husband; the overwhelming consciousness of loneliness and desolation; the tragic difficulty experienced in conveying the body to its last resting place; the unutterable agony with which she "laid the mool' on his yellow hair," and "turned about awa' to gae;" and the unconquerable strength of her affection for her "lovely knight," which even death could not vanquish—all these elements in the tragedy are depicted with a graphic and realistic power which has seldom been surpassed.

The scene of this tragedy is in the immediate neighbourhood of St. Mary's Loch. In the preface to this ballad in the *Border Minstrelsy*, Scott states that it was " obtained from recitation in

the Forrest of Ettrick, and is said to relate to the execution of
Cockburn of Henderland, a Border freebooter, hanged over the
gate of his own tower by James V, in the course of that memor-
able expedition, in 1529, which was fatal to Johnnie Armstrong,
Adam Scott of Tushielaw, and many other marauders." The
grave of *Perys Cockburn* and his wife *Marjory* is on a wooded
knoll on the banks of a small stream which joins the Meggat
near St. Mary's Loch, but it would appear that this ballad is in
no way applicable to this famous freebooter. Aytoun asserts
that it is only a skilful adaptation of an old English ballad
called "The Lady turned Serving-Man," which is printed in the
third volume of Percy's *Reliques*. He says :—"The first three
stanzas are transferred almost verbatim ; and I observe, more-
over, that in the two last, the adapter has borrowed lines from
'Helen of Kirkconnel' and 'The Twa' Corbies.' I cannot,
therefore, hold it to be ancient in its present shape, and with
reference to the incident to which Sir Walter Scott refers. Mr
Kinloch has given a Scottish version of the English ballad,
entitled 'Sweet Willie,' which has undergone the change to be
expected. No doubt there are several instances of ballads being
current, under slightly altered forms, both in England and
Scotland ; but in no case have I found the coincidence so close
as here ; and the fact that lines are also taken from extant and
undoubted Scottish ballads, seems to me a farther proof that
the 'Lament' can only be regarded as a cento." Such
criticism, however, in no way affects the literary excellences of
the ballad.

MY love he built me a bonny bower,
And clad it a' wi' lilye flour,
A brawer bower ye ne'er did see,
Than my true love he built for me.

There came a man, by middle day,
He spied his sport, and went away,
And brought the King that very night,
Who brake my bower and slew my knight.

He slew my knight, to me sae dear;
He slew my knight, and poin'd his gear;
My servants all for life did flee,
And left me in extremitie.

I sew'd his sheet, making my mane;
I watch'd the corpse myself alane;
I watch'd his body night and day;
No living creature came that way.

I took his body on my back,
And whiles I gaed, and whiles I sat;
I digg'd a grave, and laid him in,
And happ'd him with the sod sae green.

But think na ye my heart was sair,
When I laid the moul' on his yellow hair ;
O think na ye my heart was wae,
When I turn'd about, away to gae ?

Nae living man I'll love again,
Since that my lovely knight is slain,
Wi' ae lock of his yellow hair,
I'll chain my heart for evermair.

ALLAN RAMSAY.

ALLAN RAMSAY was born Oct. 15, 1686, in the village of Leadhills, Lanarkshire. On his father's side he was descended from the Ramsays of Dalhousie, a fact which gave the poet considerable satisfaction, as is evidenced by the lines:

> " Dalhousie, of an auld descent—
> My chief, my stoupe, my ornament !"

His father was superintendent of the lead mines owned by Lord Hopetoun. His mother was of English descent, the daughter of a Derbyshire gentleman who had been brought to

Leadhills to introduce some improvements in the art of mining. He was quite young when his father died, and not long after his mother married a Mr Crichton, a small landholder in Lanarkshire. Allan was educated in the parish school, and before he left he was able to read Horace " faintly in the original." He was apprenticed to a wig-maker in Edinburgh,—an occupation which most of his biographers are pleased to distinguish from that of a barber. His vocation, which he was sometimes humourously pleased to describe as that of a " skull thacker," was by no means uncongenial to the poet. He followed it long after the term of his apprenticeship had expired. Ultimately he became a bookseller, and started the first circulating library in Scotland. His writings are voluminous, his best known production being the " Gentle Shepherd," an exquisite pastoral, much read by former generations, and still admired by every true lover of poesy. He was prosperous in business, in this respect presenting a pleasing contrast to the vast majority of the votaries of the Muse. He died at Edinburgh, January 7th, 1758, in the seventy-third year of his age, and was buried in Greyfriars' Churchyard.

His poems on Yarrow are not of a particularly high order. He has not succeeded in catching the spirit of Yarrow and its surroundings ; but they possess an interest all their own, coming as they do from his pen, and that too at a period long anterior to the time when Wordsworth and Scott were destined to throw around the vale that bright halo of romance in which it is now enshrined.

MARY SCOTT.

Happy's the love which meets return,
When in soft flames souls equal burn;
But words are wanting to discover,
The torments of a hopeless lover.

Ye registers of heav'n, relate,
If, looking o'er the rolls of fate,
Did you there see, mark'd for my marrow?
Mary Scott, the flower of Yarrow?

Ah, no! her form's too heav'nly fair,
Her love the gods above must share,
While mortals with despair explore her,
And at a distance due adore her.

O, lovely maid! my doubts beguile,
Revive and bless me with a smile;
Alas! if not you'll soon debar a
Sighing swain the banks of Yarrow.

Be hush, ye fears! I'll not despair,
My Mary's tender as she's fair;
Then I'll go tell her all my anguish,
She is too good to let me languish.

With success crown'd I'll not envy
The folks who dwell above the sky;
When Mary Scott's become my marrow,
We'll make a paradise of Yarrow.

THE ROSE IN YARROW.

'Twas summer, and the day was fair,
Resolv'd awhile to fly from care,
Beguiling thought, forgetting sorrow,
I wander'd o'er the braes of Yarrow ;
Till then despising beauty's power,
I kept my heart, my own secure ;
But Cupid's dart did there deceive me,
And Mary's charms do now enslave me.

Will cruel love no bribe receive ?
No ransome take for Mary's slave ?
Her frowns of rest and hope deprive me ;
Her.lively smiles like light revive me.
No bondage may with mine compare,
Since first I saw the charming fair :
This beauteous flower, this rose of Yarrow,
In nature's gardens has no marrow.

Had I of heaven but one request,
I'd ask to lie in Mary's breast ;
There would I live or die with pleasure,
Nor spare this world one moment's leisure;
Despising kings and all that's great,
I'd smile at court's and courtier's fate ;
My joy complete on such a marrow,
I'd dwell with her and live on Yarrow.

But tho' such I ne'er should gain,
Contented still I'll wear my chain,
In hopes my faithful heart may move her,
For leaving life I'll always love her.
What doubts distract a lover's mind?
That breast, all softness, must prove kind;
And she shall yet become my marrow
The lovely, beauteous Rose of Yarrow.

WILLIAM HAMILTON.

———◆———

WILLIAM HAMILTON, of Bangour, was born of an ancient and wealthy Ayrshire family in the year 1704. His poetic genius asserted itself at an early age. Before he was twenty he had contributed several poems to Allan Ramsay's renowned *Tea-table Miscellany*. He was a man of fine culture, and of the most elegant manners; was highly popular with the aristocracy of his native county, and won for himself the appellation of "the elegant and amiable Hamilton." Like the majority of young men of that age, he had strong Jacobite sympathies; and, as happened in numerous other cases, he had to "bear the brunt" of his loyalty to the Stuarts. When the battle of Culloden finally determined the fate of the Pretender, he was fain to seek a refuge among the wild fastnesses of the Highlands. Here he wandered for a considerable time, undergoing great privations, until ultimately he succeeded in making his escape to France. After living in exile for some time, his friends brought influence to bear upon the government in his favour, with the result that he was restored to his country, and to the paternal estate which he had forfeited. His health was never robust. He died, after a lingering illness in Lyons, France, on March 25th, 1754, in the fiftieth year of his age.

The first edition of his poems was published, without his name or consent, in Glasgow, in the year 1748. The first *genuine* edition was published by his friends in 1760—with a portrait by Strange. The best and most complete edition of his poems, edited by James Paterson, appeared in 1850.

His reputation as a poet may be said to rest mainly on his exquisite lyric, " The Braes of Yarrow." Many of his other poems reveal qualities of a high order, but this production is of such distinguished merit as to completely put all his other effusions into the shade. It is highly probable that his poems as a whole may be forgotten, and pass into oblivion, but as long as Yarrow possesses charms for the poetic mind, and as long as the heart is susceptible of pure and lofty emotion, so long will " The Braes of Yarrow," be read, and sung, and admired.

THE BRAES OF YARROW.

A.   Busk ye, busk ye, my bonny, bonny bride;
    Busk ye, busk ye, my winsome marrow !
Busk ye, busk ye, my bonny, bonny bride,
    And think nae mair on the braes of Yarrow.

B.   Where gat ye that bonny, bonny bride ?
    Where gat ye that winsome marrow ?
I gat her where I darena weel be seen,
    Pu'ing the birks on the braes of Yarrow.

Weep not, weep not, my bonny, bonny bride ;
    Weep not, weep not, my winsome marrow !
Nor let thy heart lament to leave
    Pu'ing the birks on the braes of Yarrow.

B.   Why does she weep, thy bonny, bonny bride?
         Why does she weep, thy winsome marrow?
     And why dare ye nae mair weel be seen,
         Pu'ing the birks on the braes of Yarrow?

A.   Lang maun she weep, lang maun she, maun she weep,
         Lang must she weep with dool and sorrow,
     And lang maun I nae mair weel be seen
         Pu'ing the birks on the braes of Yarrow.

     For she has tint her lover, lover dear,
         Her lover dear, the cause of sorrow;
     And I hae slain the comliest swain
         That e'er pu'd birks on the braes of Yarrow.

     Why runs the stream, O Yarrow, Yarrow, red?
         Why on thy braes heard the voice of sorrow?
     And why yon melancholious weeds,
         Hung on the bonny birks of Yarrow?

     What's yonder floats on the rueful, rueful flude?
         What's yonder floats? O, dool and sorrow!
     'Tis he, the comely swain I slew
         Upon the doolful braes of Yarrow.

     Wash, O wash his wounds, his wounds in tears,
         His wounds in tears of dool and sorrow,
     And wrap his limbs in mourning weeds,
         And lay him on the braes of Yarrow.

Then build, then build, ye sisters, sisters sad,
   Ye sisters sad, his tomb with sorrow,
And weep around in waeful wise,
   His helpless fate on the braes of Yarrow.

Curse ye, curse ye, his useless, useless shield,
   My arm that wrought the deed of sorrow,
The fatal spear that pierced his breast,
   His comely breast, on the braes of Yarrow.

Did I not warn thee not to, not to lo'e,
   And warn from fight? but to my sorrow;
Ower rashly bauld, a stronger arm
   Thou mett'st, and fell on the braes of Yarrow.

Sweet smells the birk, green grows, green grows the grass,
   Yellow on Yarrow's braes the gowan,
Fair hangs the apple frae the rock,
   Sweet the wave of Yarrow flowin'.

Flows Yarrow sweet? as sweet, as sweet flows Tweed,
   As green its grass, its gowan as yellow,
As sweet smells on its braes the birk,
   The apple from its rocks as mellow.

Fair was thy love, fair, fair indeed thy love,
   In flow'ry bands thou did'st him fetter;
Though he was fair, and weel beloved again,
   Than me he never lov'd thee better.

Busk ye, then busk, my bonny bonny bride,
　　Busk ye, busk ye, my winsome marrow,
Busk ye, and lo'e me on the banks of Tweed,
　　And think nae mair on the braes of Yarrow.

C.　How can I busk a bonny bonny bride,
　　How can I busk a winsome marrow,
How lo'e him on the banks of Tweed,
　　That slew my love on the braes of Yarrow?

O Yarrow fields, may never, never rain,
　　Nor dew thy tender blossoms cover,
For there was basely slain my love,
　　My love, as he had not been a lover.

The boy put on his robes, his robes of green,
　　His purple vest, 'twas my ain sewing,
Ah! wretched me! I little, little kenn'd,
　　He was in these to meet his ruin.

The boy took out his milk-white, milk-white steed,
　　Unheedful of my dule and sorrow,
But ere the to-fall of the night,
　　He lay a corpse on the braes of Yarrow.

Much I rejoic'd that woful, woful day;
　　I sang, my voice the woods returning;
But lang ere night the spear was flown
　　That slew my love, and left me mourning.

F

What can my barbarous, barbarous father do,
   But with his cruel rage pursue me?
My lover's blood is on thy spear;
   How canst thou, barbarous man, then woo me?

My happy sisters may be, may be proud,
   With cruel and ungentle scoffin',
May bid me seek on Yarrow's braes
   My lover nailed in his coffin.

My brother Douglas may upbraid, upbraid,
   And strive with threatening words to move me;
My lover's blood is on thy spear,
   How canst thou ever bid me love thee?

Yes, yes, prepare the bed, the bed of love,
   With bridal sheets my body cover,
Unbar, ye bridal maids, the door,
   Let in the expected husband-lover.

But who the expected husband, husband is?
   His hands, methinks, are bathed in slaughter,
Ah me! what ghastly spectre's yon,
   Comes, in his pale shroud, bleeding after?

Pale as he is, here lay him, lay him down,
   O lay his cold head on my pillow;
Take aff, take aff these bridal weeds,
   And crown my careful head with willow.

Pale tho' thou art, yet best, yet best belov'd,
   O could·my warmth to life restore thee!
Ye'd lie all night between my breasts;
   No youth lay ever there before thee.

Pale, pale, indeed, O lovely, lovely youth!
   Forgive, forgive so foul a slaughter,
And lie all night between my breasts;
   No youth shall ever lie there after.

A.   Return, return, O mournful, mournful bride,
     Return and dry thy useless sorrow,
Thy lover heeds nought of thy sighs;
     He lies a corpse on the braes of Yarrow.

ALISON RUTHERFORD.

THE authoress of what is supposed to be the earliest version of "The Flowers of the Forest" was a Miss Rutherford, daughter of Robert j Rutherford, of Fernilee, the scion of an old Border House, Rutherford of Hundalee, and

was born at Fernilee House, in Selkirkshire, in 1712. She became the wife of Patrick Cockburn, advocate, youngest son of Adam Cockburn, the Lord-Justice Clerk of Scotland. Her famous song was first printed in 1765, but was written at a considerably earlier period. Allan

Cunningham gives the following account of the circumstances which led to its composition. "It is said that a young gentleman who had lost his way among the pastoral vales and hills of Selkirkshire came at last in sight of a young shepherd seated by a stream, watching his flocks and playing on his pipe. Many wild and original tunes were played by the gifted shepherd, and his wondering auditor had the skill and the cunning to carry away one of the sweetest airs of this Selkirkshire Orpheus. He had next the good fortune to meet with Miss Rutherford, and the rustic air was married to very elegant verse. Such is the story which, once told, has often been repeated."

This song, like Miss Elliot's, has been associated with Flodden, but many competent authorities affirm that it does not refer to this sorrowful episode in the history of Scotland, and are disposed to attribute its inspiration to a less tragic source. Be this as it may, the song is one of the finest in the language, and is likely long to retain its well-deserved popularity.

THE FLOWERS OF THE FOREST.

I'VE seen the smiling of Fortune beguiling,
　I've tasted her favours, and felt her decay :
Sweet is her blessing, and kind her caressing,
　But soon it is fled—it is fled far away.

I've seen the forest adorn'd of the foremost,
　With flowers of the fairest both pleasant and gay ;
Full sweet was their blooming, their scent the air perfuming,
　But now are they wither'd, and a' wede awae.

I've seen the morning with gold the hills adorning,
    And the red storm roaring, before the parting day:
I've seen Tweed's silver streams, glittering in the sunny beams,
    Turn drumly and dark, as they roll'd on their way.

O fickle Fortune ! why this cruel sporting?
    Why thus perplex us poor sons of a day?
Thy frowns cannot fear me, thy smiles cannot cheer me,
    Since the flowers of the forest are a' wede awae.

JEAN ELLIOT.

O F the life of the authoress of this exquisitely pathetic ballad not much is known. She was born at Minto, the family seat, in the year 1727. She died at Mount Teviot, her brother's residence, in 1805. She is described as possessing "a sensible face, a slender, well-shaped figure. In manner, grave and reserved to strangers. In her conversation she made no attempts at wit, and, though possessed of imagination, she never allowed it to entice her from the strictest rules of veracity. She had high aristocratic notions, which she took no pains to conceal."

Professor Veitch has described the circumstances which led to the composition of this song. He says:—"When a young woman Miss Elliot was riding home in a carriage after night-fall to Minto House from a party with her brother Gilbert. The conversation turned on Flodden, that disaster which left a sadness on the hearts of Scotchmen and Scotch women for three hundred years. The brother suggested to the sister, not perhaps believing much in her capacity for it, that this was a fitting subject for a song. She leant backwards in the carriage, and there under the shadow of the nightfall with the old refrain, 'The Flowers of the Forest are a' wede awae,' sounding in her ear, as a stray echo from the past, and mingling in fancy with the scenery of her life and love, and under the kindling of her true human heart, she framed 'The Flowers of the Forest,' that immortal lyric, in which simple natural pictures of joy and sadness are so exquisitely blended and contrasted, in which pathos of heart and patriotism of spirit, and a music that echoes the plaintive sough of the Border Waters, passed, as it were spontaneously, into one consummate outburst of song."

It may be said that these two songs on the "Flowers of the Forest" do not properly belong to the poetical literature of Yarrow, but we would remind our readers that in the time of Flodden, Yarrow was really the central river of "Ettricke Foreste," and beyond doubt contributed its quota of heroes to that memorable catastrophe.

THE FLOWERS OF THE FOREST.

I'vE heard them lilting, at the ewe-milking,
  Lasses a' lilting, before dawn of day ;
But now they are moaning on ilka green loaning ;
  The flowers of the forest are a' wede awae.

At bughts, in the morning, nae blythe lads are scorning ;
  Lasses are lonely, and dowie, and wae ;
Nae daffing, nae gabbing, but sighing and sabbing ;
  Ilk ane lifts her leglin, and hies her awae.

In har'st, at the shearing, nae youths now are jeering ;
  Bandsters are runkled, and lyart or gray ;
At fair, or at preaching, nae wooing, nae fleeching ;
  The flowers of the forest are a' wede awae.

At e'en, in the gloaming, nae younkers are roaming
  'Bout stacks with the lasses at bogle to play;
But ilk maid sits dreary, lamenting her deary—
  The flowers of the forest are weded awae.

Dool and wae for the order, sent our lads to the Border !
  The English for ance, by guile wan the day:
The flowers of the forest, that fought aye the foremost,
  The prime of our land, are cauld in the clay.

We'll hear nae mair lilting, at the ewe-milking;
  Women and bairns are heartless and wae,
Sighing and moaning on ilka green loaning—
  The flowers of the forest are a' wede awae.

JOHN LOGAN.

———◆———

JOHN LOGAN, the author of the following well-known song, "The Braes o' Yarrow," was born at Soutra, Mid-Lothian, in the year 1748. He was educated at Gosforth, and afterwards sent to Edinburgh University, with a view to his entering the ministry. After completing his curriculum he was engaged, on the recommendation of Dr Blair, by Sir John Sinclair of Ulbster, as tutor to his eldest son. He does not seem, however, to have remained long in this situation. In 1770 he edited the poetical remains of his friend and class mate, Michael Bruce.

To Logan we are indebted for some of the most popular of the Paraphrases appointed to be sung in public worship :— "O God of Jacob," "Few are thy days and full of woe," "Behold the mountain of the Lord," "O happy is the man who hears," &c., &c., are from his pen. He was ordained to the parish of South Leith in 1773, and enjoyed the reputation of an able and eloquent preacher. His ministerial career was somewhat suddenly brought to a close by his publication of the tragedy of "Runnimede," which was performed in the Edinburgh Theatre. This gave mortal offence to his worthy parishioners, who induced him to resign his charge. He died of a lingering illness at the early age of forty.

THE BRAES OF YARROW.

THY braes were bonnie, Yarrow stream !
　When first on thee I met my lover;
Thy braes how dreary, Yarrow stream !
　When now thy waves his body cover !
For ever now, O Yarrow stream !
　Thou art to me a stream of sorrow;
For never on thy banks shall I
　Behold my love, the flower of Yarrow.

He promised me a milk-white steed,
　To bear me to his father's bowers ;
He promised me a little page,
　'To squire me to his father's towers ;
He promised me a wedding ring,—
　The wedding day was fix'd to-morrow ;—
Now he is wedded to his grave,
　Alas ! his watery grave in Yarrow !

Sweet were his words when last we met,
　My passion I as freely told him,
Clasp'd in his arms, I little thought
　That I should never more behold him !
Scarce was he gone, I saw his ghost ;
　It vanished with a shriek of sorrow ;
Thrice did the water-wraith ascend,
　And gave a doleful groan through Yarrow.

His mother from the window look'd,
   With all the longing of a mother;
His little sister weeping walk'd
   The greenwood path to meet her brother:
They sought him east, they sought him west,
   They sought him all the Forest thorough;
They only saw the cloud of night,
   They only heard the roar of Yarrow!

No longer from thy window look,
   Thou hast no son, thou tender mother!
No longer walk, thou lovely maid!
   Alas! thou hast no more a brother!
No longer seek him east or west,
   And search no more the Forest thorough;
For, wandering in the night so dark,
   He fell a lifeless corse in Yarrow.

The tears shall never leave my cheek,
   No other youth shall be my marrow,
I'll seek thy body in the stream,
   And then with thee I'll sleep in Yarrow.
The tear did never leave her cheek,
   No other youth became her marrow;
She found his body in the stream,
   And now with him she sleeps in Yarrow.

WILLIAM WORDSWORTH.

WILLIAM WORDSWORTH was born at Cockermouth, Cumberland, on the 7th April, 1770. He was the second son of John Wordsworth, attorney, and land agent to the first Earl of Lonsdale. His first school was in Penrith, where his parents had gone to reside, but in course of time he was sent to Hawkshead School, in Lancashire, where he completed his early education. His environment was peculiarly favourable to the development of his poetical genius. The influence which the magnificent scenery in that region exercised over his youthful imagination has been finely described in *The Prelude* where he sings :—

> "Was it for this
> That one, the fairest of all rivers, loved
> To blend his murmurs with my nurse's song,
> And from his alder shades and rocky falls,
> And from his fords and shallows, sent a voice
> That flowed along my dreams? For this didst thou,
> O Derwent! winding among grassy holms
> Where I was looking on, a babe in arms,
> Make ceaseless music that composed my thoughts
> To more than infant softness, giving me
> Amid the fretful dwellings of mankind
> A foretaste, a dim earnest, of the calm
> That nature breathes among the hills and groves."

> "Fair seed time had my soul, and I grew up
> Fostered alike by beauty and by fear :
> Much favoured in my birth-place, and no less
> In that beloved vale to which ere long
> We were transplanted—there were we let loose
> For sports of wider range."

> "Ye Presences of Nature in the sky
> And on the earth! ye visions of the hills!
> And souls of lonely places! can I think
> A vulgar hope was yours when ye employed
> Such ministry, when ye through many a year
> Haunting me thus among my boyish sports,
> On caves and trees, upon the woods and hills,
> Impressed upon all forms the characters
> Of danger or desire ; and thus did make
> The surface of the universal earth
> With triumph and delight, with hope and fear,
> Work like a sea ?"

In 1787 Wordsworth entered St. John's College, Cambridge, where he remained for four years. He did not distinguish himself as a student. He says that he felt that he was not for that place, nor for that hour. But he was far from being idle. He read much, and thought deeply on those themes that lay nearest to his own heart. After taking his bachelor's degree, he and a fellow-student made a pedestrian tour in France, then deeply agitated by the early fervours of the great Revolution. He seems to have had considerable sympathy with the Girondists, and was on terms of intimacy with some of the party, a circumstance that might have involved him in serious trouble had not pecuniary difficulties compelled him to return to England shortly before his friends were sent in a body to the scaffold. This episode in his career was not without important results. He was strongly opposed to the war waged against France, and it was only after England entered on a life and death struggle with the military despotism of Napoleon that he became reconciled to the attitude of his own country. The rebound was unmistakable. He became by-and-by a pronounced and uncompromising conservative, though it is but fair to admit that he was singularly free from mere class prejudice, which is sometimes no inconsiderable factor in determining political relationships.

He first came before the public as an author in 1793, when he published two poems, entitled, "An Evening Walk—Addressed to a Young Lady;" and "Descriptive Sketches taken during a Pedestrian Tour among the Alps." These productions, though abounding in refined and original observations of Nature, are not otherwise specially distinguished, and give but a faint indication of the superlative quality of his genius. They did not fail, however, to excite admiration in certain quarters. Coleridge, then a student in Cambridge, was profoundly impressed by them, and felt assured that their author was certain ultimately to secure for himself a distinguished place among the poets of the country. At this time Wordsworth was in great pecuniary difficulties. His friends urged him to enter the Church, but this was a step which on no consideration was he prepared to take. He was on the point of proceeding to London to earn a livelihood by writing political articles, but an event occurred which upset his plans, and changed the whole aspect of his affairs. A friend and admirer of the poet, Raisley Calcot—his name is worthy of honourable mention—died, and left Wordsworth a legacy of £800, in order, as he expressly stated, that leisure might for some years be allowed for the undisturbed development of his powers. This gift could not have come more opportunely. The sum was not large, but to a man of Wordsworth's simple habits it was sufficient to meet his requirements for many years.

He had become intimate with Coleridge—a friendship fraught with important results—and in 1797 he removed, in company with his sister Dorothy, a life-long companion, to Alfoxden, in Somersetshire, in order that they might have frequent intercourse, Coleridge being then established at Nether-Stowey, a place some three miles distant. The first fruit of this literary friendship was the famous *Lyrical Ballads*, published by the redoubtable "Amos Cottle," who formed such an admirable target for Byron's satirical wit. This venture may be described as a conspicuous failure, but this fact in no way ruffled the imperturbable serenity of Wordsworth's spirit. He doubtless felt that the poet, not of a day, but of all time, had need of patience, as his claims were not likely to meet with speedy recognition on the part of the multitude. He must create the taste by which he is to be appreciated. This feeling had much to do with the remarkable *sang-froid* which Wordsworth exhibited under the most scathing criticisms. The *Edinburgh Review*, edited by Jeffrey, was then a terror to all aspirants to literary fame, and many a writer must have felt that his future largely depended on the judgment passed upon him by this "Arbiter of Fate." Not a few were driven almost to madness by the manner in which the offspring of their literary genius were torn limb from limb, and mutilated past all hope either of recognition or resuscitation. But Wordsworth was oblivious to such outbursts of violent and misguided passion. He was laughed at and ridiculed in a fashion which would have extinguished most men; but he had only a feeling of pity for his critics—could not help being sorry for them on account of their blindness and stupidity. He went calmly on his way, fully satisfied in his own mind that he had something to teach that it would be good for them to know, and he felt convinced that the day was coming when he would be listened to and appreciated. His serene self-confidence was not doomed to be rudely shaken. As he came to be more widely known his merits as a poet began to be recognised by many of the best minds in the country. His shortcomings in some directions were sufficiently apparent. He aimed at conferring a dignity

G

on certain subjects, which, from the nature of the case, were incapable of being dignified. His " Peter Bell," for example, notwithstanding its profound merits, is made ridiculous by the fact that the hero of it is an incorrigible donkey. Had Wordsworth only been more richly endowed with the divine gift of humour, he would have been saved from absurdities of this kind ; but when the most has been made of such imperfections the fact remains that few poets in any age or country have laid mankind under a deeper debt of obligation. He has shown that Nature is susceptible of a poetic as well as of a scientific interpretation, and he has brought the minds of men back to this fountain of inspiration. He has not the distinguished credit of being the pioneer in this new movement, for Cowper and Burns had already led the way, but he carried out to the fullest extent the great principles which they were the first to bring into prominence. In this matter Wordsworth has frankly acknowledged his indebtedness to Burns in those ever memorable lines :—

> " I mourned with thousands, but as one
> More deeply grieved, for *he* was gone
> Whose light I hailed when first it shown,
>   And showed my youth
> How verse may build a princely throne
>   On humble truth."

These two great poets differ, however, in this, that Burns almost invariably uses Nature as the counterfoil of his feeling or passion,—this is strikingly apparent in such songs as " Ye Banks and Braes o' Bonnie Doon " and " Flow Gently, Sweet Afton,"—whereas Wordsworth, generally speaking, seeks to discover the secret of Nature, and rests satisfied with the knowledge thus acquired. In other words, he loves Nature for her own sake.

His three poems on Yarrow occupy a foremost place in the poetical literature of the valley. It is difficult to determine which of the three is most worthy of admiration, as each may be likened to a priceless gem in a different setting. In " Yarrow Unvisited " the poet displays a gay bantering spirit. Though on the very confines· of the enchanted stream, he will not be induced to turn aside and view it. His words of scorn awaken a painful sensation in the bosom of his " winsome Marrow," but he heeds not, feeling that there is a kind of compensation in the thought that "earth has something yet to show." In " Yarrow Visited," and " Yarrow Re-visited," Wordsworth has embalmed in imperishable verse the spirit of the vale. The latter poem is pervaded by a feeling of sadness, due in great part to the fact that Scott, who was with him on this occasion, was in failing health, and was about to leave for the Continent, to return ere long to die.

YARROW UNVISITED.

———◆———

Composed, 1803; Published, 1807.

———◆———

MISS WORDSWORTH, in her journal dated Sept. 18, 1803, gives the following account of the circumstances which led to the composition of this poem. "We left the Tweed when we were within about a mile and a half or two miles of Clovenford, where we were to lodge. Turned up the side of a hill, and went along sheep-grounds till we reached the spot—a single stone house, without a tree near it or to be seen from it. On our mentioning Mr Scott's name, the woman of the house showed us all possible civility, but her slowness was really amusing. I should suppose it a house little frequented, for there is no appearance of an inn. Mr Scott, who, she told me, was a very clever gentleman, 'goes there in the fishing season;' but indeed Mr Scott is respected everywhere; I believe that by favour of his name one might be hospitably entertained throughout all the borders of Scotland. We dined and drank tea—did not walk out, for there was no temptation, a confined barren prospect from the window.

"At Clovenford, being so near Yarrow, we could not but think of the possibility of going thither, but came to the conclusion of reserving the pleasure for some future time, in consequence of which, after our return, William wrote the poem which I shall here transcribe."

YARROW UNVISITED.

From Stirling Castle we had seen
The mazy Forth unravelled ;
Had trod the banks of Clyde, and Tay,
And with the Tweed had travelled ;
And when we came to Clovenford,
Then said my *"winsome Marrow,"*
" Whate'er betide, we'll turn aside,
And see the Braes of Yarrow."

" Let Yarrow folk, *frae* Selkirk town,
Who have been buying, selling,
Go back to Yarrow, 'tis their own ;
Each maiden to her dwelling !
On Yarrow's banks let herons feed,
Hares couch, and rabbits burrow !
But we will downward with the Tweed,
Nor turn aside to Yarrow.

" There's Gala Water, Leader Haughs,
Both lying right before us ;
And Dryborough, where with chiming Tweed
The lint-whites sing in chorus ;
There's pleasant Tiviotdale, a land
Made blithe with plough and harrow :
Why throw away a needful day
To go in search of Yarrow ?

What's Yarrow but a river bare,
That glides the dark hills under?
There are a thousand such elsewhere
As worthy of your wonder."
—Strange words they seemed of slight and scorn;
My True-love sighed for sorrow;
And looked me in the face, to think
I thus could speak of Yarrow!

" Oh! green," said I, "are Yarrow's holms,
And sweet is Yarrow flowing!
Fair hangs the apple frae the rock,
But we will leave it growing.
O'er hilly path, and open Strath,
We'll wander Scotland thorough;
But, though so near, we will not turn
Into the dale of Yarrow.

" Let beeves and home-bred kine partake
The sweets of Burn-mill meadow;
The swan on still St. Mary's Lake
Float double, swan and shadow!
We will not see them; will not go,
To-day, nor yet to-morrow;
Enough if in our hearts we know
There's such a place as Yarrow.

" Be Yarrow stream unseen, unknown!
It must, or we shall rue it:
We have a vision of our own;
Ah! why should we undo it?

The treasured dreams of times long past,
We'll keep them, winsome Marrow!
For when we're there, although 'tis fair,
'Twill be another Yarrow!

" If Care with freezing years should come,
And wandering seem but folly,—
Should we be loth to stir from home,
And yet be melancholy ;
Should life be dull, and spirits low,
'Twill soothe us in our sorrow,
The earth has something yet to show,
The bonny holms of Yarrow!"

YARROW VISITED.

Composed, 1814; Published, 1820.

WORDSWORTH had come up the Tweed to Traquair, where he spent a night with Mr Nicol, the minister of the parish. There Hogg joined him, and the next day they walked across to Yarrow by Paddy Slacks, and the Gordon Arms. The first view which the poet got of the famous stream was from the height, a few yards to the west of the old farmhouse of Mount Benger.

YARROW VISITED.

Sept. 1814.

And is this—Yarrow ?—*This* the stream
Of which my fancy cherished,
So faithfully, a waking dream ?
An image that hath perished !
O that some Minstrel's harp were near,
To utter notes of gladness,
And chase this silence from the air,
That fills my heart with sadness !

Yet why?—a silvery current flows
With uncontrolled meanderings;
Nor have these eyes by greener hills
Been soothed, in all my wanderings.
And, through her depths, Saint Mary's Lake
Is visibly delighted;
For not a feature of those hills
Is in the mirror slighted.

A blue sky bends o'er Yarrow vale,
Save where that pearly whiteness
Is round the rising sun diffused,
A tender hazy brightness;
Mild dawn of promise! that excludes
All profitless dejection;
Though not unwilling here to admit
A pensive recollection.—

Where was it that the famous Flower
Of Yarrow Vale lay bleeding?
His bed perchance was yon smooth mound
On which the herd is feeding:
And haply from this crystal pool,
Now peaceful as the morning,
The Water-wraith ascended thrice—
And gave his doleful warning.

Delicious is the Lay that sings
The haunts of happy Lovers,
The path that leads them to the grove,
The leafy grove that covers:

And Pity sanctifies the Verse
That paints, by strength of sorrow,
The unconquerable strength of love ;
Bear witness, rueful Yarrow.

But thou, that did'st appear so fair
To fond imagination,
Dost rival in the light of day
Her delicate creation :
Meek loveliness is round thee spread,
A softness still and holy ;
The grace of forest charms decayed,
And pastoral melancholy.

That region left, the vale unfolds
Rich groves of lofty stature,
With Yarrow winding through the pomp
Of cultivated nature ;
And, rising from those lofty groves,
Behold a Ruin hoary !
The shattered front of Newark's Towers,
Renowned in Border story.

Fair scenes for childhood's opening bloom,
For sportive youth to stray in ;
For manhood to enjoy his strength ;
And age to wear away in !
Yon cottage seems a bower of bliss,
A covert for protection
Of tender thoughts, that nestle there—
The brood of chaste affection.

How sweet, on this autumnal day,
The wild-wood fruits to gather,
And on my True-love's forehead plant
A crest of blooming heather !
And what if I enwreathed my own !
'Twere no offence to reason ;
The sober Hills thus deck their brows
To meet the wintry season.

I see—but not by sight alone,
Loved Yarrow, have I won thee ;
A ray of fancy still survives—
Her sunshine plays upon thee !
Thy ever-youthful waters keep
A course of lively pleasure ;
And gladsome notes my lips can breathe,
Accordant to the measure.

The vapours linger round the Heights,
They melt, and soon must vanish ;
One hour is theirs nor more is mine —
Sad thoughts which I would banish,
But that I know, where'er I go,
Thy genuine image, Yarrow !
Will dwell with me—to heighten joy,
And cheer my mind in sorrow.

YARROW REVISITED.

Composed during a Tour in Scotland in the Autumn of 1831.

WORDSWORTH has thus described his second visit to the district:—" On Tuesday morning Sir Walter Scott accompanied us and most of the party to Newark Castle on the Yarrow. When we alighted from the carriages he walked pretty stoutly, and had great pleasure in revisiting those his favourite haunts. Of that excursion the verses 'Yarrow Revisited' are a memorial. Notwithstanding the romance that pervades Sir Walter's works and attaches to many of his habits, there is too much pressure of fact for these verses to harmonise as much as I could wish with other poems. On our return in the afternoon we had to cross the Tweed directly opposite Abbotsford. The wheels of our carriage grated upon the pebbles in the bed of the stream that there flows somewhat rapidly; a rich but sad light of rather a purple than a golden hue was spread over the Eildon Hills at that moment; and, thinking it probable that it might be the last time Sir Walter would cross the stream, I was not a little moved, and expressed some of my feelings in the sonnet beginning—'A trouble, not of clouds, or weeping rain.' At noon on Thursday we left Abbotsford, and in the morning of that day Sir Walter and I had a serious conversation tête-a-tête, when he spoke with gratitude of the happy life which upon the whole he had led. He had written in my daughter's album, before he came into the breakfast-room that morning, a few stanzas as addressed to her, and, while putting the book into her hand, in his own study, standing by his desk, he said to her in my presence—'I should not have done anything of this kind but for your father's sake: they are probably the last verses I shall ever write.' They show how much his mind was impaired, not by the strain of thought but by the execution, some of the lines being imperfect, and one stanza wanting corresponding rhymes : one letter, the initial S had been omitted in the spelling of his own name.   In this interview also it was that, upon my expressing a hope of his health being benefited by the climate of the country to which he was going, and by the interest he would take in the classic remembrances of Italy, he made use of the quotation from ' Yarrow Unvisited' as recorded by me in the *Musings of Aquapendente* six years afterwards."

YARROW REVISITED.

The gallant Youth, who may have gained,
  Or seeks a " winsome Marrow,"
Was but an Infant in the lap
  When first I looked on Yarrow ;
Once more, by Newark's Castle-gate
  Long left without a warder,
I stood, looked, listened, and with Thee,
  Great Minstrel of the Border !

Grave thoughts ruled wide on that sweet day,
   Their dignity installing
In gentle bosoms, while sere leaves
   Were on the bough, or falling;
But breezes played, and sunshine gleamed—
   The forest to embolden;
Reddened the fiery hues, and shot
   Transparence through the golden.

For busy thoughts the Stream flowed on
   In foamy agitation;
And slept in many a crystal pool
   For quiet contemplation:
No public and no private care
   The freeborn mind enthralling,
We made a day of happy hours,
   Our happy days recalling.

Brisk Youth appeared, the Morn of youth,
   With freaks of graceful folly,—
Life's temperate Noon, her sober Eve,
   Her Night not melancholy;
Past, present, future, all appeared
   In harmony united,
Like guests that meet, and some from far,
   By cordial love invited.

And if, as Yarrow, through the woods
   And down the meadow ranging,
Did meet us with unaltered face,
   Though we were changed and changing;

If, *then*, some natural shadows spread
    Our inward prospect over,
The soul's deep valley was not slow
    Its brightness to recover.

Eternal blessings on the Muse,
    And her divine employment!
The blameless Muse, who trains her Sons,
    For hope and calm enjoyment,
Albeit sickness, lingering yet,
    Has o'er their pillow brooded ;
And Care waylays their steps—a Sprite
    Not easily eluded.

For thee, O Scott ! compelled to change
    Green Eildon-hill and Cheviot
For warm Vesuvio's vine-clad slopes ;
    And leave thy Tweed and Tiviot
For mild Sorento's breezy waves ;
    May classic Fancy, linking
With native Fancy her fresh aid,
    Preserve thy heart from sinking !

O ! while they minister to thee
    Each vying with the other,
May Health return to mellow Age,
    With Strength her venturous brother ;
And Tiber, and each brook and rill
    Renowned in song and story,
With unimagined beauty shine,
    Nor lose one ray of glory !

For Thou. upon a hundred streams,
   By tales of love and sorrow,
Of faithful love, undaunted truth,
   Hast shed the power of Yarrow;
And streams unknown, hills yet unseen,
   Wherever they invite Thee,
At parent Nature's grateful call,
   With gladness must requite Thee.

A gracious welcome shall be thine,
   Such looks of love and honour
As thy own Yarrow gave to me
   When first I gazed upon her;
Beheld what I had feared to see,
   Unwilling to surrender
Dreams treasured up from early days,
   The holy and the tender.

And what, for this frail world, were all
   That mortals do or suffer,
Did no responsive harp, no pen,
   Memorial tribute offer?
Yea, what were mighty Nature's self?
   Her features, could they win us,
Unhelped by the poetic voice
   That hourly speaks within us?

Nor deem that localised Romance
   Plays false with our affections;
Unsanctifies our tears—made sport
   For fanciful dejections:

Ah, no ! the visions of the past
   Sustain the heart in feeling
Life as she is—our changeful Life,
   With friends and kindred dealing.

Bear witness, Ye, whose thoughts that day
   In Yarrow's groves were centred ;
Who through the silent portal arch
   Of mouldering Newark enter'd ;
And clomb the winding stair that once
   Too timidly was mounted
By the " last Minstrel " (not the last !)
   Ere he his Tale recounted.

Flow on for ever, Yarrow Stream !
   Fulfil thy pensive duty,
Well pleased that future Bards should chant
   For simple hearts thy beauty ;
To dream-light dear while yet unseen,
   Dear to the common sunshine,
And dearer still, as now I feel,
   To memory's shadowy moonshine !

JAMES HOGG.

J AMES HOGG, the Ettrick Shepherd, was born at Ettrick-
hall, a small farm-house in the immediate vicinity of
Ettrick Kirk. The date of his birth is uncertain. He was
wont to affirm that he had been born on the 25th January—
"a ne'er to be forgotten day"—1772; but his baptism is
recorded in the Session records of the parish as having taken

place on the 9th October, 1770. How he came to regard himself as two years younger than he really was we cannot say; but it is not difficult to understand his partiality for the 25th of January. As a young man he was fired with the noble ambition of becoming the successor of Burns, and he may have thought that to begin life on this particular date was a good augury of future fame.

His family was of an ancient lineage—his ancestors having occupied the farm of Fauldshope for over 400 years—but at the time of the poet's birth they were in comparatively humble circumstances. In early life his father had followed the occupation of shepherd, and it would have been well for him had he been content " to wear the crook and plaid." He took the farm of Ettrickhall, thinking he would improve his position; but in a few years he lost every penny of his hard won earnings, and had the mortification of seeing his " goods and chattels " exposed for sale to meet the claims of his numerous creditors. This sad change in the family fortunes may account for the fact that Hogg was allowed to grow up almost entirely uneducated. His school life extended over a few months—six or eight at most—when he learned to read the Shorter Catechism and the Proverbs of Solomon. He was sent to herd a neighbour's cows when a mere child, and received for wages " a pair of shoes and a ewe lamb." By the time he reached manhood he had been in the service of at least a dozen different masters.

One of the most potent factors in the formation of his

H2

character and development of his genius was the influence of
his mother—a woman of great intelligence and force of
character. From her lips Sir Walter Scott heard, for the first
time, many of those grand old ballads which he has immortalized
in his *Minstrelsy.* Her prediction that when they were printed
they would cease to be sung, has been strikingly verified. She
could tell no end of legendary tales and traditional stories, and
was wont to amuse and interest her children by speaking to
them about brownies, kelpies, witches, fairies, etc., and thus
keep them quiet while she was engaged in the onerous duties
of her household. Brought up under such influences, it is
not surprising that Hogg should ultimately have become, in
an especial sense, "the Poet of the Fairies." In referring
to his friendship with Sir Walter Scott, he gives beautiful
expression to his sense of indebtedness to his mother's
influence and teaching in the following lines :—

> " Blessed be his generous heart for aye,
> He told me where the relic lay ;
> Pointed my way with ready will,
> Afar on Ettrick's wildest hill ;
> Watched my first step with curious eye,
> And wondered at my minstrelsy ;
> *He little weaned a parent's tongue*
> *Such strains had o'er my cradle sung.*"

We are told that he acquired the art of penmanship—*lucus
a non lucendo*—by trying to make the characters of the
alphabet on the big slate stones on the hillside!

When he was about twenty years of age he entered the
service of Mr Laidlaw, farmer in Blackhouse, a wild and
romantic region on the Douglas Burn, a few miles north of

St. Mary's Loch. Here he spent some of the happiest, and—from an intellectual point of view—most important years of his life. He now began to write verses, and felt immensely flattered when he heard them sung by the servants as they sat round the cheery peat fire of an evening. His method of composition was peculiar. Seating himself among the heather, with a small ink bottle attached to a piece of twine, fastened to a hole in his waistcoat, and with a stump of a pen, he wrote out carefully and laboriously —for his hand often took the cramp, notwithstanding that he had his coat off and his sleeves well buckled up—the verses which he had been carefully conning over in his mind.

One day when out on the hill "simmering his lambs" he met with Jock Scott, a "half-witted creature," well known in the Border country, who had a remarkable faculty for reciting poetry. Burns had been in his grave for more than a year, yet, strange to relate, the Ettrick Shepherd had never heard of him. His astonishment, therefore, may be more easily imagined than described when Scott began to recite that immortal epic, "Tam o' Shanter." Big tears of joy and surprise coursed down his quivering cheek. The poem had to be repeated again and again until every word of it had been got by heart. From Scott's lips he also learned the tragic history of the Ayrshire bard. His resolution was instantly formed. He determined to become the successor of Burns. He felt sure that "he could tell more stories, and sing more songs than ever ploughman could in the world."

What was to hinder him becoming a great poet? It was thus he reasoned with himself as he pictured in imagination the great future which he felt sure lay before him. This resolution on Hogg's part has often been referred to by his critics as an indication of inordinate vanity; yet it must be frankly admitted that, while he came far short of the goal set before him, he has written several pieces which Burns might well have been proud to claim.

His first published song, "Donald M'Donald," attained great popularity. The poet once heard it sung in a theatre in Wigan, and when it had been *encored*, he told a burly Yorkshireman who was sitting beside him that he was the author. This statement only called forth an incredulous smile—the worthy Englishman telling Hogg's landlady afterwards that he took him for a half-crazed Scotch pedlar!

He had strong Jacobitic sympathies, and rendered admirable service to the cause of literature by the publication of the *Jacobitic Relics of Scotland*, a work in two vols., which entailed upon him immense labour and research. He went into the Highlands that he might gather from the lips of the people themselves every ballad and song relating to the fortunes of the "ill-starred" Bonnie Prince Charlie. The difficulties he had to encounter were frequently of a vexatious character. "The Highlanders were suspicious of him. Donald would eye him with a suspicious look and say, 'Ohon, man, you surely haif had very less to do at home; and so you want to get some of the songs of the poor repellioners from me, and then you will give me up to King Shorge and be hanged! Ho, no, that will never do.'"

It was the publication of *The Queen's Wake*, however, which finally established Hogg's reputation as a poet. It took the world completely by surprise. Men wondered to hear a simple untaught shepherd sing so eloquently and so well. The general feeling was not inappropriately expressed by a Mr Dunlop, from Ettrick, who happened to meet the author in the High Street of Edinburgh a few days after the publication of the book. "Your *Queen's Wake*," he said, "has cheated me out of a night's sleep. Wha wad hae thocht that there was sae muckle in that sheep's head of yours!" The plan of this poem is natural and simple. Queen Mary, who has recently landed on our shores, proclaims a Royal Wake, at which all minstrels, Highland and Lowland, are summoned to appear to contend with each other in poetical competition. His own appearance on this occasion provokes considerable merriment. The very sound of his name excites to laughter:—

> " But when the bard himself appeared,
> The ladies smiled, the courtiers sneered,
> For such a simple air and mein
> Before a court had never been.
> A clown he was bred in the wild,
> And late from native moors exiled,
> In hopes his mellow mountain strain
> High favour trom the great would gain.
> Poor wight! he little weaned how hard
> For poverty to earn regard.
> Dejection o'er his visage ran,
> His coat was bare, his colour wan,
> His forest doublet darned and torn,
> His shepherd plaid all rent and worn,
> Yet dear the symbols to his eye,
> Memorials of a time gone bye."

But he was not abashed. Nature had been kindly. His lot had been cast in one of her most favoured spots, on the banks of the Yarrow, and near by St. Mary's Loch and the "lonely Lowes"—no fitter home on earth than this, for the poet.

"Oft had he viewed when morning rose,
The bosom of the lonely Lowes,
Ploughed far by many a downy keel,
Of wild duck and of vagrant teal;
Oft thrilled his heart at close of even
To see the dappled vales of heaven,
With many a mountain, moor, and tree,
Asleep upon the St. Mary."

"Kilmeny"—a poem of superlative excellence—is incomparably the finest piece in the *Queen's Wake*. In the *Noctes Ambrosianæ* Wilson has given a characteristic account of the way in which this wonderful poem was composed.

"*Shepherd.*—My imagination, sir, a' at ance wafted me awa' intil the laneliest spat amang a' the hills whare my childhood played—and amang the broom-bushes and the brackens there, I was beginnin when you reca'd me by that rap on the table, to sink awa' back again intil the dream o' dreams!

"*North.*—The dream o' dreams?

"*Shepherd.*—Ay, sir—The dream, sir, in which I saw Kilmeny? For though I wrote down the poem on the sclate in the prime o' manhood, anither being than mysel' did in verity compose or creawte it, sir, ae day when I was lyin a' by mysel in that laneliest spat, wi' but twa-three sheep aside me, ae linty and nae mair; but oh! how sweetly the glad cretur sang! and after *that some other cretur nor me* had composed or creawted it, she keepit whisper, whisperin the words far within my ears, till memory learned them a' off by heart as easy as the names o' Christian creturs that we meet wi' on Sabbaths at the kirk; and frae that genie-haunted hour, known now through a' braid Scotland is the Ettrick Shepherd—

"*North.*—Britain and America——

"*Shepherd.*—But for many obscure years a nameless man, or kent by the name o' Jamie amang my simple compeers, 1 carried bonny Kilmeny for ever in the arms o' my heart, kissin her shut een whan she sleepit, and her lips as calm as the lips o' death, but as sweet as them o' an undying angel!

"*North.*—And such was the origin of the finest Pastoral Lyric in our tongue!

"*Shepherd.*—Sic indeed, sir, was its origin. For my sowl, ye see, sir, had fa'n into a kind o' inspired dwaum—and the Green Leddy o' the Forest, nae less than the Fairy Queen hersel, had stown out frae the land o' peace on my slumber; and she it was that stooped down, and wi' her ain lily-haun shedding frae my forehead the yellow hair, left a kiss upon my temples, just where the organ o' imagination or ideality lies; and at the touch arose the vision in which

'Bonny Kilmeny gaed up the glen,'
and frae which you, sir, in your freendship say, that I became ane o' the Immortals."

Had Hogg written nothing but Kilmeny, he would still have been entitled to a high place among the great poets of our country. Ticknor, the famous American scholar, met him on one occasion in London, and after conversing with him he felt astonished that such a plain, uneducated, and apparently unsophisticated shepherd, could have produced such a masterpiece of poetical genius. Yet the fact remains that in this poem the Ettrick Shepherd has struck a note on his simple lyre which will vibrate through many centuries.

Hogg's social habits have frequently been severely commented on. He has been described by a reviewer as a "Boozing Buffoon." This statement, we have good grounds for saying, is not only overdrawn, but maliciously inaccurate. We have frequently conversed with those who knew the poet intimately, and their unanimous testimony is that he was thoroughly temperate in his habits. Doubtless, the times in which he lived were, in this respect, very different from our own. Then it was considered no disgrace to imbibe somewhat freely, but no one is entitled to judge a former generation by the standard of to-day. To do so is to violate the fundamental principle of all true and honest criticism. He was no doubt eminently social, as most great men are, but when the worst has been said, it simply amounts to this, that he conformed to the customs of his age, and of the society in which he moved. He spent many jovial hours in the company of Wilson, and other literary friends, under the hospitable roof of the far-famed " Tibbie Shiel." On one occasion, it is said, that his thirst was so intense that he was constrained to ask his genial hostess to "bring in the Loch !" But surely this does not prove him to have been an inebriate !

The truth regarding Hogg's social habits has, perhaps, never been more accurately described than in the well-known passage in the *Noctes*, where he is represented as saying—" What's this I was intendin to say ? Ou, ay ! It was that you ken ma character by havin studied it in sic moods and seasons. Noo, I was a few minutes ago describin a roasted guse—wi' a' the zest o' a glutton, whose imagination was kindled by his pallet. And at that moment as sincere was I as ever you beheld me when standin by the side of some great loch, and gazing on the sun sinking behind the mountains. But what care I, sir, for a' the guses that ever was roasted ? No ae single strae.

Gie me a bit cheese and bread when I am hungry, and I will say grace ower't, sittin by some spring amang the hills, wi' as gratefu' a heart as ever yearned in a puir sinner's breist towards the Giver o' a' mercies. Nae objections hae I—why sud I?—to a jug o' toddy; especially, sir, sittin cheek-by-jowl wi' auld Christopher. But mony and mony a day o' drivin rain, and blastin sleet and driftin snaw, hae I been out frae morn till nicht amang the hills—ay, sir, frae nicht till morn—a' thro' the wild sughing hours o' the mirk nichts o' winter, without ever thinking o' spirits in the shape o' whisky ony mair than if in this weary world there never had been ae single still. Sumphs —base insolent sumphs—say I, sir, that dare to insult the shepherd at his Glenlivet wi' the king o' men. Has the aipple o' my ee, sir, tint ae hue o' its brichtness, or shows it one blood-shot streak or stain o' intemperance? Has the aipple o' my cheek, sir, tint ae hue o' its ruddiness, or shows it one blotch or pimple o' excess, either o' eatin' or drinking?—the Cockney cooards and calumniawtors!"

His vanity, we are also told, was excessive; but even in this respect he compares not unfavourably with his contemporaries. He was certainly less self-conscious than either Byron or Keats, or for that matter, Wordsworth, humble as he was to all outward seeming, and in Hogg's case there was more excuse for such a failing. He was all but uneducated, and consequently the distinction he attained as a man of letters was due to his genius and indomitable perseverance. From the obscurity of his shepherd-life, he suddenly burst upon the world as a great poet. He could number among his friends many of the fore-most men of his age, in learning, intellect, and social position. In these circumstances his vanity, such as it was, need surprise no one. It would have been a marvel had he not at times felt unduly elated. The wonder really is, all things considered, that he was so well able to keep his feet on the ground.

Carlyle has left an interesting sketch of him. He says: —"Hogg is a little red-skinned, stiff rack of a body, with quite the common air of an Ettrick shepherd, except that he has a highish, though sloping brow (among his yellow grizzled hair), and two clear little beads of blue or grey eyes that sparkle, if not with thought, yet with animation. Behaves himself easily and well; speaks Scotch, and mostly narrative absurdity (or even obscenity) therewith. Appears in the mingled character of zany or raree show. All bent on bantering him, especially Lockhart; Hogg walking through it as if unconscious, or almost flattered. His vanity seems to be immense, but also his good nature. I felt interest for the poor herd-body; wondered to see him blown hither from his sheep-folds, and how, quite friend-less as he was, he went along cheerful, mirthful, and musical. I do not well understand this man; his significance is perhaps considerable. His poetic talent is authentic, yet his intellect seems of the weakest; his morality also limits itself to the precept 'be not angry.' Is the charm of this poor man to be found herein, that he *is* a real product of nature, and able to speak naturally, which not one in a thousand is? An un-conscious talent, though of the smallest, emphatically naïve.

Once or twice in singing (for he sang of his own) there was an emphasis in poor Hogg's look—expressive of feeling—almost of enthusiasm. The man is a very curious *specimen*. Alas, he is a *man*; yet how few will so much as treat him like a *specimen*, and not like a mere wooden Punch or Judy."

The closing years of Hogg's life were spent in comparative ease and comfort. His books commanded a ready sale, though he did not always reap the full harvest of his literary labours. He had abundant leisure at command, after he left the farm of Mount Benger, and many a happy day he spent in fishing in the Yarrow and its tributaries, or shooting over the hills and moors in the neighboorhood of Altrive Lake—a small farm which the Duke of Buccleuch generously gave him at a merely nominal rent. Despite his many misfortunes, he rarely ever succumbed to a feeling of despondency. He says:—" I never knew either man or woman who has been so uniformly happy as I have been; which has been partly owing to a good constitution, and partly from the conviction that a heavenly gift, conferring the powers of immortal song, was inherent in my soul. Indeed so uniformly smooth and happy has my married life been, that in a retrospect I cannot distinguish one part from another save by some remarkably good days of fishing, shooting, and curling on the ice." He had also the satisfaction of knowing—and this doubtless had something to do with his general buoyancy of feeling—that his talents were thoroughly appreciated by all classes in the community. His merits were instantly recognised, and from the beginning to the close of his literary career, he received on the part of the public an amount of recognition which many a writer of more distinguished ability might well have envied.

His last meeting with Sir Walter Scott has been thus described by Professor Veitch :—" Scott had sent him word that he was to pass down the Yarrow from Drumlanrig, on his way to Abbotsford. The carriage stopped at the small inn, the Gordon Arms, and here the shepherd met Sir Walter. They walked down the road past Mount Benger, Sir Walter leaning heavily on Hogg's arm, and walking very feebly. The Shepherd noticed the change, bodily and mental, in the great man, whom he honoured, almost worshipped. There was some talk, not of a very clear kind, but kindly and affectionate. It was exactly twenty-nine years before that Hogg, a young man, had met Scott in his mother's cottage at Ettrick Hall, when the editor of the *Minstrelsy* was sowing the seed that had ripened during those intervening years into that glorious golden harvest of poem and romance—as rich an outcome of one man's life as the world had ever seen. Here appropriately enough, in beloved Yarrow,—dear to Hogg, and dearest vale on earth to Scott,—the two poets whom Yarrow herself had quickened and nourished, parted for the last time on earth. One cannot help feeling that this touching incident gives a new interest to the spot in the vale where they met and parted, and adds another to the many sacred associations which cluster round the name of Yarrow."

Five years after, in 1835, the shepherd-poet was laid to rest under the shadow of Ettrick Pen, and near the old homestead where he was born.

> " Long has that harp of magic tone,
>   To all the minstrel world been known ;
>   Who has not heard her witching lays
>   Of Ettrick banks and Yarrow braes ?
>   But that sweet bard who sang and played
>   Of many a feat and Border raid,
>   Of many a knight and lovely maid,
>   When forced to leave his harp behind
>   Did all her tuneful chords unwind ;
>   And many ages past and came
>   Ere man so well could tune the same."

Hogg was a voluminous author. His best known poetical works are *The Queen's Wake, The Mountain Bard, Mador of the Moor, The Forest Minstrel, The Poetic Mirror, Poetical Tales and Ballads,* &c. Among his prose works, *The Brownie of Bodsbeck,"* *The Shepherd's Calendar, and The Siege of Roxburgh*, are the best known.

Wordsworth's well-known poem on Hogg's death may here appropriately be given :—

> When first, descending from the moorlands,
>   I saw the stream of Yarrow glide
> Along a bare and open valley,
>   The Ettrick Shepherd was my guide.
>
> When last along its banks I wandered,
>   Through groves that had begun to shed
> Their golden leaves upon the pathways,
>   My steps the Border Minstrel led.
>
> The mighty Minstrel breathes no longer,
>   'Mid mouldering ruins low he lies ;
> And death upon the braes of Yarrow,
>   Has closed the Shepherd-poet's eyes :
>
> Nor has the rolling year twice measured,
>   From sign to sign, its steadfast course,
> Since every mortal power of Coleridge
>   Was frozen at its marvellous source ;

The rapt One of the god-like forehead,
  The heaven-eyed creature sleeps in earth ;
And Lamb, the frolic and the gentle,
  Has vanished from his lonely hearth.

Like clouds that rake the mountain summits,
  Or waves that own no curbing hand,
How fast has brother followed brother
  From sunshine to the sunless land !

Yet I, whose lids from infant slumber
  Were earlier raised, remain to hear
A timid voice, that asks in whispers,
  " Who next will droop and disappear ? "

Our haughty life is crowned with darkness,
  Like London, with its own black wreath,
On which with thee, O ! Crabbe, forth-looking
  I gazed from Hampstead's breezy heath.

As if but yesterday departed,
  Thou too art gone before ; but why
O'er ripe fruit, seasonably gathered
  Should frail survivors heave a sigh.

Mourn rather for that holy Spirit.
  Sweet as the spring, as ocean deep ;
For Her who, ere her summer faded,
  Has sunk into a breathless sleep.

No more of old romantic sorrows,
  For slaughtered youth or love-lorn maid !
With sharper grief is Yarrow smitten,
  And Ettrick mourns with her their Poet dead.

DESCRIPTION OF MOUNT BENGER.

Oft from yon height I loved to mark,
Soon as the morning roused the lark,
And woodlands raised their raptured hymn,
That land of glory spreading dim ;
While slowly up the awakening dale
The mists withdrew their fleecy veil,
And tower, and wood, and winding stream,

Were brightening in the golden beam.
Yet where the westward shadows fell,
My eye with fonder gaze would dwell,
Though wild the view, and brown and bare ;
Nor castled halls, nor hamlets fair,
Nor range of sheltering woods, were there,
Nor river's sweeping pride between,
To give *expression* to the scene.
There stood a simple home, where swells
The meady sward to moory fells,
A rural dwelling thatched and warm,
Such as might suit the upland farm.
A honeysuckle clasped the sash,
Half shaded by the giant ash ;
And there the wall-spread apple-tree
Gave its white blossoms to the bee,
Beside yon sheltering clump of ash,
Which screens below the boiling pool
With pebbled bottom clear and cool,
Where often, from the shelving brim,
We launched on sedgy sheaf to swim.

BY A BUSH.

By a bush on yonder brae
  Where the airy Benger rises,
Sandy tuned his artless lay ;
Thus he sung the lee-lang day :

" Thou shalt ever be my theme,
    Yarrow, winding down the hollow,
With thy bonny sister stream
    Sweeping through the broom so yellow.
        On these banks thy waters lave,
        Oft the warrior found a grave.

" Oft on thee the silent wain
    Saw the Douglas' banners streaming ;
Oft on thee the hunter train
Sought the shelter'd deer in vain ;
Oft, in thy green dells and bowers
    Swains have seen the fairies riding ;
Oft the snell and sleety showers
    Found in thee the warrior hiding.
        Many a wild and bloody scene
        On thy bonnie banks have been.

" Now the days of discord gane,
    Henry's kindness keeps us cheery ;
While his heart shall warm remain,
Dule will beg a hauld in vain.
Bloodless now in many hues,
    Flow'rets bloom, our hills adorning ;
There my Jenny milks her ewes,
    Fresh an' ruddy as the morning,
        Mary Scott could ne'er outvie
        Jenny's hue an' glancing eye.

" Wind, my Yarrow, down the howe,
　　Forming bows o' dazzling siller;
Meet thy titty yont the knowe;
Wi' my love I'll join like you.
Flow my Ettrick, it was thee,
　　Into life wha first did drap me.
Thee I've sung, an' when I dee
　　Thou wilt lend a sod to hap me:
　　　　Passing swains shall say, and weep,
　　　　Here our Shepherd lies asleep."

WILL AND DAVIE:

A SCOTTISH PASTORAL.

Where Yarrow pours her silver billow
Through bowers of birch, and brakes of willow;
Where loud the grouse crows on the fell,
And sweet the thrush sings in the dell;
Where milk-white flocks unnumbered lie,
And mirth laughs keen in every eye;
And plenty smiles from day to day,
Beneath Buccleuch's indulgent sway;
Two friendly shepherds, blithe and young.
Oft on the greensward sat and sung,
Or scoured the lofty fells together,
And brushed the red flower from the heather.

12

One morn they tuned, by dawn of day,
On Bowerhope Law the rural lay;
For such a scene that lay was meet—
As wildly gay, as simply sweet;
The great may even lend an ear
Wild Yarrow's mountain strains to hear.

DAVIE.

Ah, Will, these purple heather blooms,
That round us shed their light perfumes,
These sparkling gems of crystal dew,
That morning sky so mild and blue,
Have raised my heart to such a height,
I breathe so pure, I feel so light,
'Gainst all the reasons you can bring
I must and will my matin sing.
Cheer up your heart, for once be gay;
Screw on your flute and join the lay.

WILL.

Ah, Shepherd, cease; your idle strain
Adds sharpness to my bosom's pain.
How can ye pour that strain so airy,
That trifling, idle, wild vagary;
Nor sadly once reflect with me
On what has been, and what may be?

" As little heeds the lark on high,
The watchful falcon hovering nigh,
But flickering his kind mate above,
He trills his matin song of love.

Ah, reckless bird, that lively strain
Thy mate shall never hear again !
The spoiler tears thy panting breast,
And all forsaken is thy nest."

Cease, Shepherd, cease—the case is yours ;
The sky of Britain threatening lowers !
Else, let your strain be soft and slow,
And every fall a note of woe.

DAVIE.

How can I strike one plaintive sound
While nature smiles so sweet around ?
See how our lambs, in many a skein,
Are dancing on the daisied green ;
Their pliant limbs they keenly brace,
Strained in the unambitious race ;
Till gruff old wedders, blithe to see
The young things skip so merrily,
With motley antics join the throng,
And bob and caper them among.

The plover whistles in the glen,
The tewit tilts above the fen ;
Even the hoarse curlew strains her throat,
And yelps her loudest, liveliest note :
The rural joy then must I shun,
So ripened by the rising sun ?

No—while my bosom beats so high,
Responsive to a lovely eye
That pierced it with a gilded arrow,
I'll sing of love, of joy, and Yarrow.

I'll sing that rural scene before me ;
That shady world of placid glory.
See how the afer vibrates o'er
The lofty front of brown Clockmore ;
Beyond Carlevon's rocky crest
The drowsy moon sinks pale to rest ;
An angel shade of silken green
O'erveils the cliffs of wild Loch Skene ;
While Border Cheviot, blue and high,
Melts like a shadow on the sky.

From proud Mount Benger's top, the sun
His airy course has scarce begun ;
His orient cheek is resting still
Upon the grey cairn on the hill.
The scarlet curtain of the sky,
A wreathed and waving canopy,
Sweels like the dew on mountain flower
Or frost-work on the southland shower.

The Yarrow, like a baldrick thrown
Loose on the vale, lies bent and lone ;
A silver snake of every dye
That gilds the mountain, tincts the sky ;
And slowly o'er her verdant vales
A cobweb veil of vapour sails.

Saint Mary holds her mirror sheen,
To moorland gray and mountain green ;
To speckled schell-fowl hovering nigh,
To milky swan and morning sky :
Their phantom cliffs hang trembling low,
And hoary thorns inverted grow.

Her purple bosom sleeps as still
As sunbeam on the silent hill,
No curling breeze across it strays,
No sportful eddy o'er it plays,
Save where the wild duck wanders slow,
Or dark trout spreads his waxing O.

Look to the east—'tis shadow all,
Crowned by yon broad and dazzling ball.
Turn westward—mountain, glen, and wold,
Are all one blaze of burning gold !

Ah, God of nature ! such a scene,
So grand, so lovely, so serene,
Bears the free soul on rapture's wing,
Before thy diamond throne to sing ;
Above yon sky's celestial blue,
To gaze on glories ever new ;
And list the strains of angel song
From angel harps that pour along,
By fragrant breezes softly driven
O'er suns that sand the floors of heaven.

The enraptured youth now ceased to sing;
But still on ether's waving wing,
From echo's cave was borne along
Thy dying measures of the song:
With eye entranced, and head declined,
They listened to the waving wind—
Hung on the cliff-born fairly lay,
Till the last quaver died away.

THE LASSIE OF YARROW.

"What makes my heart beat high,
What makes me heave the sigh,
When yon green den I spy,
      Lonely and narrow?
Sure on your bracken lea,
Under the hawthorn tree,
Thou hast bewitched me,
      Lassie of Yarrow!"

"Yon bracken den so lone,
Rueful I ponder on;
Lad, though my vow ye won,
      'Twas to deceive thee.
Sore, sore I rue the day
When in your arms I lay,
And swore by the hawthorn gray,
      Never to leave thee."

" Mary, thy will is free ;
All my fond vows to thee
Were but in jest and glee ;
    Could'st thou believe me ?
I have another love
Kind as the woodland dove ;
False to that maid to prove,
    Oh, it would grieve me !"

Mary's full eye so blue,
Mild as the evening dew,
Quick from his glance withdrew,
    Soft was her sighing ;
Keen he the jest renewed,
Hard for his freedom sued—
When her sweet face he viewed,
    Mary was crying.

" Cheer thee," the lover said,
" Now thy sharp scorn repaid,
Never shall other maid
    Call me her marrow.
Far sweeter than sun or sea,
Or aught in this world I see,
Is thy love-smile to me,
    Lassie of Yarrow !"

ST. MARY OF THE LOWES.

O lone St. Mary of the waves,
   In ruin lies thine ancient aisle,
While o'er thy green and lowly graves,
   The moorcocks bay, and plovers wail :
   But mountain spirits on the gale,
Oft o'er thee sound the requiem dread ;
   And warrior shades, and spectres pale,
Still linger by the quiet dead.

Yes, many a chief of ancient days
   Sleeps in thy cold and hallow'd soil ;
Hearts that would thread the forest maze,
   Alike for spousal or for spoil ;
   That wist not, ween'd not, to recoil
Before the might of mortal foe,
   But thirsted for the Border broil,
The shout, the clang, the overthrow.

Here lie those who, o'er flood and field,
   Were hunted as the osprey's brood,
Who braved the power of man, and seal'd
   Their testimonies with their blood :
   But long as waves that wilder'd flood,
Their sacred memory shall be dear,
   And all the virtuous and the good
O'er their low graves shall drop the tear.

Here sleeps the last of all the race
  Of these old heroes of the hill,
Stern as the storm in heart and face :
  Gainsaid in faith or principle.
  Then would the fire of heaven fill
The orbit of his faded eye ;
  Yet all within was kindness still,
Benevolence and simplicity.

GRIEVE, thou shalt hold a sacred cell
  In hearts with sin and sorrow toss'd ;
While thousands, with their funeral knell,
  Roll down the tide of darkness, lost ;
  For thou wert Truth's and Honour's boast,
Firm champion of Religion's sway !
  Who knew thee best revered thee most,
Thou emblem of a former day !

Here lie old Border bowmen good ;
  Ranger and stalker sleep together,
Who for the red-deer's stately brood
  Watch'd, in despite of want and weather,
  Beneath the hoary hills of heather ;
Even Scotts, and Kerrs, and Pringles, blended
  In peaceful slumbers, rest together,
Whose fathers there to death contended.

Here lie the peaceful, simple race,
  The first old tenants of the wild,
Who stored the mountains of the chase
  With flocks and herds—whose manners mild

Changed the baronial castles, piled
In every glen, into the cot,
   And the rude mountaineer beguiled,
Indignant, to his peaceful lot.

Here rural beauty low reposes ;
   The blushing cheek, and beaming eye,
The dimpling smile, the lip of roses,
   Attracters of the burning sigh,
   And love's delicious pangs, that lie
Enswathed in pleasure's mellow mine :
   Maid, lover, parent, low and high,
Are mingled in thy lonely shrine.

And here lies one—here I must turn
   From all the noble and sublime,
And, o'er thy new but sacred urn,
   Shed the heath flower and mountain-thyme,
   And floods of sorrow, while I chime
Above thy dust one requiem.
   Love was thine error, not thy crime,
Thou mildest, sweetest, mortal gem !

For ever hallow'd be thy bed,
   Beneath the dark and hoary steep ;
Thy breast may flowerets overspread,
   And angels of the morning weep
   In sighs of heaven above thy sleep,
And tear-drops of embalming dew ;
   Thy vesper hymn be from the deep,
Thy matin from the ether blue !

I dare not of that holy shade,
  That's pass'd away, one thought allow ;
Not even a dream that might degrade
  The mercy before which I bow :
  Eternal God, what is it now ?
Thus asks my heart : but the reply
  I aim not, wish not, to foreknow,
'Tis veiled within eternity.

But, oh, this earthly flesh and heart
  Still cling to the dear form beneath,
As when I saw its soul depart,
  As when I saw it calm in death :
  The dead rose, the funereal wreath
Above the breast of virgin snow,
  Far lovelier than in life and breath,
I saw it then, and see it now.

That her fair form shall e'er decay,
  One thought I may not entertain ;
As she was on her dying day,
  To me she ever will remain.
  When Time's last shiver o'er his reign
Shall close this scene of sin and sorrow,
  How calm, how lovely, how serene,
That form shall rise upon the morrow !

Frail man ! of all the arrows wounding
  Thy mortal heart, there is but one
Whose poison'd dart is so astounding,
  That bear it, cure it, there can none.

It is the thought of beauty won,
To love in most supreme degree,
    And, by the hapless flame undone,
Cut off from nature and from thee !

SIR WALTER SCOTT.

T HERE are few names more closely associated with Yarrow
than that of the "Great Minstrel of the Border."
Indeed, it may be said that Scott was, in an especial sense,
a son of Yarrow. He was a descendent, by both parents,
of ancestor's whose home was in the "Dowie Dens." On his

father's side he was related in a direct line to Mary Harden Scott, the far-famed *Flower of Yarrow;* and on the mother's to John Rutherford, who, for a period of nineteen years, was the faithful and much respected minister of the parish. The Latin inscription on Rutherford's tombstone—a mural tablet in the north wall of the church—is both curious and interesting. The following is a translation:—

"To the memory of John Rutherford, minister of the Church of Yarrow, most upright and most vigilant; and of Robert, his son, in his fourth year; Christiana Shaw, his mourning wife, was careful to erect this monument. Died May 7, 1710, in the 19 year of his ministry, and 69 year of his age.

"Thou wert a faithful pastor, a beloved brother, a sure friend, a gentle master, a genial husband and father.

"Having resigned the gift of an upright and pure life, thou hast yielded to the fates; thy years passed happily, O thrice blessed! thy fame is above the high hills and green banks of Yarrow, thy soul above the stars!"

Often did Sir Walter, when residing in Ashiestiel, then in the parish of Yarrow, walk over the hills to this old Kirk in the Forest "to worship," as he used to say, "at the shrine of his ancestors." The Rutherfords were a talented family. Professor Rutherford, son of the minister, and grandfather of Scott, was a notable man in his day, and contributed not a little towards the fame which the medical schools in Edinburgh have so long and justly enjoyed. It has sometimes been said that it was through the Rutherfords Scott inherited his extraordinary genius. Be this as it may, it is a significant and highly interesting fact that he had an ancestral connection with the romantic vale which his genius has done so much to render famous in all parts of the world. There may, therefore, be more than a mere element of association to account for the feeling expressed with touching pathos in the lines :—

> " By Yarrow's stream still let me stray,
> Though none should guide my feeble way ;
> Still feel the breeze down Ettrick break,
> Although it chill my withered cheek."

This period of Scott's life was at once the happiest and most fruitful in his long and chequered career. He was still happily free from those harassing and killing cares which the building of Abbotsford was so soon to bring upon him. He held an office which kept him in touch with the public interests of the time, and his income from this and other sources was more than sufficient to meet the wants of his household, and the numerous claims on his beneficence. His home life was unclouded. He had a young and promising family growing up around him, in whose education and training he took the keenest personal interest. His literary activity was also unbounded. He rose betimes, and the early hours were religiously consecrated to painstaking, yet rapid, composition. During this bright and busy period he wrote *The Lay of the Last Minstrel, Marmion, The Lady of the Lake,* and *Waverley*—four of the most brilliant productions which his fertile pen has given to the world. Lockhart regards *Marmion* as the greatest of all his poems—a judgment that subsequent criticism has more than substantiated. The *Lay* and *Marmion* are both full of local colouring. The scene of the former is laid at Newark, an old Border Castle or " Keep," still in an excellent state of preservation, standing on the banks

K

of the Yarrow, some four miles above Selkirk, and near Bowhill, a favourite residence of the " Bold Buccleuch." The latter is a "Tale of Flodden Field," and is replete with the most graphic descriptions of Border scenery.

But Scott was no brooding recluse, buried in his books, uninterested in the life of the great world around him. He toiled hard at his desk, yet he always found plenty of time to engage in those out-of-door exercises and pastimes for which he had at once great aptitude and liking. Despite his lameness he was an excellent walker, and many a pleasant afternoon was spent in scouring the surrounding hills, followed by his faithful deerhounds, fleet of foot, quick of eye, and ever ready for the chase. Sometimes, also, he would take long rides, over into the vale of Yarrow, as far as "lone St. Mary's," where—

> " Your horse's hoof tread sounds too rude,
> So stilly is the solitude."

On such occasions he was always splendidly mounted. He was passionately fond of horses, and seems to have been more than ordinarily fortunate in his selection. *Brown Adam* (so called after one of the heroes of the Minstrelsy), was one of the famous steeds he rode at this time. We are told that he was intractable in other hands, though in his the most submissive of faithful allies. "The moment he was bridled and saddled, it was the custom to open the stable door as a signal that his master expected him, when he immediately trotted to the side of the *leaping-on-stone*, of which Scott from his lameness found it convenient to make use, and stood there, silent and motionless as a rock, until he was fairly in his seat, after which he displayed his joy by neighing triumphantly through a brilliant succession of curvettings. 'Brown Adam' never suffered himself to be backed but by his master. He broke, I believe, one groom's arm and another's leg in the rash attempt to tamper with his dignity."

These exercises were varied at certain seasons by an exciting pastime, which in these degenerate days has become illegal—(not merely *extra legal !*)—*burning the water*. The Tweed Commissioners—an august body for which the Souters of Selkirk are supposed to entertain anything but kindly feelings—had not then emerged into notoriety, and consequently no restrictions seem to have been imposed on the spearing of salmon. As every Borderer is aware, this captivating amusement is carried on under cloud of night. Armed with leister and torch, a raid is made on some famous pool where salmon are known to be plentiful. The search is highly exciting owing to the difficulty of capturing the prey, and also on account of the misadventures which so frequently befall the too eager sportsman. "This amusement of burning the water," writes Mr Skene—on one occasion when on a visit to Sir Walter—" was not without some hazard, for the large salmon generally lie in the pools, the depths of which it is not easy to estimate with precision by torch light; so that not unfrequently, when the sportsman makes a determined thrust at a fish apparently within reach, his

K2

eye has greatly deceived him, and instead of the point of the
weapon encountering the prey, he finds himself launched with
corresponding vehemence heels over head into the pool, both
spear and salmon gone, the torch thrown out by the concussion
of the boat, and quenched in the stream, while the boat itself
has receded to some distance. I remember the first time I
accompanied our friend he went right over the gunwale in this
manner, and had I not accidentally been by his side, and made
a successful grasp at the skirt of his jacket as he plunged
overboard, he must at least have had an awkward dive for it."
This interesting amusement, we may say, is still frequently
indulged in despite the statutory prohibition, but now the
adventurous sportsman must needs keep an eye on the bailiffs
as well as the salmon!

Like every great poet, Scott was eminently sociable in his
disposition. He was at home in almost every cottage and farm-
house between Tweed and Teviot, between the Eildons and
Ettrick Pen. He lived on terms of friendship with men
belonging to all classes in the community. He was warmly
attached to the noble house of Buccleuch, and enjoyed in
a rare degree the confidence of the various members of the
family. He had also an interesting neighbour in *Laird Nippy*,
of the Peel, who, as his *sobriquet* implies, was of a stingy
disposition, but withal had many excellent qualities. Despite
his worldliness he had evidently a kindly feeling towards his
distinguished neighbour, for we find that years after Scott had
settled in Abbotsford, old Nippy kept the seat on the " Sheriff's

Knowe" in good repair as a mark of his respect for Sir Walter. This, Scott once declared, was the greatest compliment he ever received. At this time also his acquaintance with James Hogg, the Ettrick Shepherd, ripened into a warm attachment. He must have felt a deep interest in the simple, untutored, egotistic, yet, withal, kindly and sociable shepherd who sang with a note as clear, musical, and spontaneous as his own "Deathless Skylark." There were times, too, when Hogg must have severely put to the test the large-heartedness of his friend. For example, when he wrote Sir Walter asking him to send a contribution to his *Poetic Mirror*, and was met for some reason or other with a blank refusal, he gave way to an outburst of passion, and wrote Scott saying—"——, Sir, I hold your friendship and literary talents in contempt!" Such incidents, however, were not without a redeeming element of humour, and, at most, only caused a slight ripple on the surface of a friendship which for many years was a source of great interest to the one, and of much advantage, both intellectually and socially, to the other. An old man, who in early life was a stable boy in Sir Walter's employment, used to say, when speaking of Hogg's visits, that the pony he rode at that time presented an extraordinary appearance. It had a long shaggy mane and tail which were evidently utter strangers to brush and comb, and moreover it frequently bore abundant traces of having been placed in too close proximity to the henery!

Among other visitors at Ashiestiel was Mungo Park, the

African traveller, whose home at Fowldshiels was only a few miles distant. Lockhart has given a deeply interesting account of Park's last visit to Scott. Towards the end of the autumn, when about to quit his country for the last time, Park paid Scott a farewell visit and slept at Ashiestiel. Next morning his host accompanied him homewards over the wild chain of hills between the Tweed and the Yarrow. Park talked much of his new scheme, and mentioned his determination to tell his family that he had business for a day or two in Edinburgh, and send them his blessing from thence, without returning to take leave. He had married not long before a beautiful and amiable woman, and when they reached the Williamhope Ridge, the autumnal mist floating slowly down the valley of the Yarrow, presented to Scott's imagination a striking emblem of the troubled and uncertain prospect which his undertaking had afforded. He remained, however, unshaken, and at length they reached the spot at which they had agreed to separate. A small ditch divided the moor from the road, and in going over it Park's horse stumbled and nearly fell. "I am afraid, Mungo," said the Sheriff, "that is a bad omen," to which he answered, "*Friets* follow those who look to them." In a few moments these two friends had parted for the last time on earth.

It would have been well had Scott contented himself in Ashiestiel—well at least for his own peace of mind—for here he spent eight bright and peaceful years—yet the troubles which the building of Abbotsford brought upon him led him to exercise his literary talents in a way that would have been impossible in other and happier circumstances. The associations of Ashiestiel are all joyful and peaceful, and the place will be visited by many for his sake as long as *Waverley* and *Marmion* are remembered.

Scott was born at Edinburgh on the 15th August, 1771, and died at Abbotsford on the 21st September, 1832.

HUSHED IS THE HARP.

["THE LAY OF THE LAST MINSTREL."—*Canto VI.*]

Hush'd is the harp—the Minstrel gone,
And did he wander forth alone?
Alone, in indigence and age,
To linger out his pilgrimage?
No :—close beneath proud Newark's tower,
Arose the Minstrel's lowly bower;

A simple hut; but there was seen
The little garden, hedged with green,
The cheerful hearth, and lattice clean.
There shelter'd wanderers, by the blaze,
Oft heard the tale of other days;
For much he loved to ope his door,
And give the aid he begg'd before.
So pass'd the winter's day; but still,
When summer smiled on sweet Bowhill,
And July's eve, with balmy breath,
Waved the blue-bells on Newark heath;
When throstles sung in Hare-head shaw,
And corn was green on Carterhaugh,
And flourished, broad, Blackandro's oak,
The aged Harper's soul awoke !
Then would he sing achievements high,
And circumstance of chivalry,
Till the rapt traveller would stay,
Forgetful of the closing day;
And noble youths, the strain to hear,
Forsook the hunting of the deer;
And Yarrow, as he rolled along,
Bore burden to the Minstrel's song.

BURNING OF ST. MARY'S KIRK.

[From "THE LAY OF THE LAST MINSTREL."—*Canto II.*]

For the Baron went on pilgrimage,
And took with him this elvish Page,

To Mary's chapel of the Lowes:
For there, beside our Ladye's lake,
An offering he had sworn to make,
   And he would pay his vows.
But the Ladye of Branksome gather'd a band
Of the best that would ride at her command;
   The trysting-place was Newark Lee.
Wat of Harden came thither amain,
And thither came John of Thirlestane,
And thither came William of Deloraine;
   They were three hundred spears and three.
Through Douglas-burn, up Yarrow stream,
Their horses prance, their lances gleam.
   They came to St. Mary's lake ere day;
   But the chapel was void, and the Baron away.
They burned the chapel for very rage,
And cursed Lord Cranstoun's Goblin-Page.

YARROW IN THE OLDEN TIME.

["MARMION"—*Introduction to Canto II.*]

The scenes are desert now, and bare,
Where flourish'd once a forest fair,
When these waste glens with copse were lined,
And peopled with the hart and hind.
Yon Thorn—perchance whose prickly spears
Have fenced him for three hundred years,
While fell around his green compeers—

Yon lonely Thorn, would he could tell
The changes of his parent dell,
Since he, so grey and stubborn now,
Waved in each breeze a sapling bough;
Would he could tell how deep the shade,
A thousand mingled branches made;
How broad the shadows of the oak,
How clung the rowan to the rock,
And through the foliage show'd his head,
With narrow leaves, and berries red;
What pines on every mountain sprung,
O'er every dell what birches hung,
In every breeze what aspens shook,
What alders shaded every brook:

"Here, in my shade," methinks he'd say.
"The mighty stag at noon-tide lay:
The wolf I've seen, a fiercer game,
(The neighbouring dingle bears his name,)
With lurching step around me prowl,
And stop, against the moon to howl;
The mountain-boar, on battle set,
His tusks upon my stem would whet;
While doe, and roe, and red-deer good,
Have bounded by, through gay green-wood.
Then oft, from Newark's riven tower,
Sallied a Scottish monarch's power:
A thousand vassals muster'd round,
With horse, and hawk, and horn, and hound;

And I might see the youth intent,
Guard every pass with crossbow bent;
And through the brake the rangers stalk,
And falc'ners hold the ready hawk ;
And foresters in green-wood trim,
Lead in the leash the gazehounds grim,
Attentive, as the bratchet's bay,
From the dark covert drove the prey,
To slip them as he broke away.
The startled quarry bounds amain,
As fast the gallant greyhounds strain ;
Whistles the arrow from the bow,
Answers the harquebuss below ;
While all the rocking hills reply,
To hoof clang, hound, and hunter's cry,
And bugles ringing lightsomely."—

Of such proud huntings, many tales
Yet linger in our lonely dales,
Up pathless Ettricke, and on Yarrow,
Where erst the outlaw drew his arrow.
But not more blithe that silvan court,
Than we have been at humbler sport ;
Though small our pomp, and mean our game,
Our mirth, dear Marriott, was the same,
Remembers't thou my greyhounds true?
O'er holt, or hill, there never flew,
From slip, or leash, there never sprang,
More fleet of foot, or sure of fang.

Nor dull, between each merry chase,
Pass'd by the intermitted space ;
For we had fair resource in store,
In Classic, and in Gothic lore:
We mark'd each memorable scene,
And held poetic talk between ;
Nor hill, nor brook, we paced along,
But had its legend, or its song.
All silent now—for now are still
Thy bowers, untenanted Bowhill !
No longer, from thy mountains dun,
The yeoman hears the well-known gun,
And, while his honest heart glows warm,
At thought of his paternal farm,
Round to his mates a brimmer fills,
And drinks " The Chieftain of the Hills !"
No fairy forms, in Yarrow's bowers,
Trip o'er the walks, or tend the flowers,
Fair as the elves whom Janet saw,
By moonlight, dance on Carterhaugh ;
No youthful Baron's left to grace
The Forest-Sheriff's lonely chase,
And ape, in manly step and tone,
The majesty of Oberon :
And she is gone, whose lovely face
Is but her least and lowest grace ;
Though if to Sylphid Queen 'twere given,
To show our earth the charms of heaven,
She could not glide along the air,
With form more light, or face more fair.

No more the widow's deafen'd ear
Grows quick, that lady's step to hear:
At noontide she expects her not,
Nor busies her to trim the cot;
Pensive she turns her humming wheel,
Or pensive cooks her orphan's meal;
Yet blesses, ere she deals their bread,
The gentle hand by which they're fed.

From Yair,—which hills so closely bind,
Scarce can the Tweed his passage find,
Though much he fret, and chafe, and toil,
Till all his eddying currents boil,—
Her long-descended lord is gone,
And left us by the stream alone.
And much I miss those sportive boys,
Companions of my mountain joys,
Just at the age 'twixt boy and youth,
When thought is speech, and speech is truth.
Close to my side, with what delight
They press'd to hear of Wallace wight,
When, pointing to his airy mound,
I call'd his ramparts holy ground!
Kindled their brows to hear me speak;
And I have smiled, to feel my cheek,
Despite the difference of our years,
Return again the glow of theirs.
Ah, happy boys! such feelings pure,
They will not, cannot, long endure;

Condemn'd to stem the world's rude tide,
You may not linger by the side;
For Fate shall thrust you from the shore,
And Passion ply the sail and oar.
Yet cherish the remembrance still,
Of the lone mountain, and the rill;
For trust, dear boys, the time will come,
When fiercer transport shall be dumb,
And you will think right frequently,
But, well I hope, without a sigh,
On the free hours that we have spent
Together, on the brown hills bent.

When, musing on companions gone,
We doubly feel ourselves alone,
Something, my friend, we yet may gain,
There is a pleasure in this pain:
It soothes the love of lonely rest,
Deep in each gentler heart impress'd.
'Tis silent amid worldly toils,
And stifled soon by mental broils;
But, in a bosom thus prepared,
Its still small voice is often heard,
Whispering a mingled sentiment,
'Twixt resignation and content.
Oft in my mind such thoughts awake,
By lone Saint Mary's silent lake;
Thou know'st it well,—nor fen, nor sedge,
Pollute the pure lake's crystal edge;

Abrupt and sheer, the mountains sink
At once upon the level brink ;
And just a trace of silver sand
Marks where the water meets the land.
Far in the mirror, bright and blue,
Each hill's huge outline you may view ;
Shaggy with heath, but lonely bare,
Nor tree, nor bush, nor brake, is there,
Save where, of land, yon slender line
Bears thwart the lake the scatter'd pine.
Yet even this nakedness has power,
And aids the feeling of the hour :
Nor thicket, dell, nor copse you spy,
Where living thing conceal'd might lie ;
Nor point, retiring, hides a dell,
Where swain, or woodman lone, might dwell ;
There's nothing left to fancy's guess,
You see that all is loneliness :
And silence aids—though the steep hills
Send to the lake a thousands rills ;
In summer tide, so soft they weep,
The sound but lulls the ear asleep ;
Your horse's hoof-tread sounds too rude,
So stilly is the solitude.

Nought living meets the eye or ear,
But well I ween the dead are near ;
For though, in feudal strife, a foe
Hath laid Our Lady's chapel low,

Yet still, beneath the hallow'd soil,
The peasant rests him from his toil,
And, dying, bids his bones be laid,
Where erst his simple fathers pray'd.

If age had tamed the passions' strife,
And fate had cut my ties to life,
Here, have I thought, 'twere sweet to dwell,
And rear again the chaplain's cell,
Like that same peaceful hermitage,
Where Milton long'd to spend his age.
'Twere sweet to mark the setting day,
On Bourhope's lonely top decay;
And, as it faint and feeble died,
On the broad lake, and mountain's side,
To say, " Thus pleasures fade away;
Youth, talents, beauty, thus decay,
And leave us dark, forlorn, and grey;"—
Then gaze on Dryhope's ruin'd tower,
And think on Yarrow's faded Flower:
And when that mountain-sound I heard,
Which bids us be for storm prepared,
The distant rustling of his wings,
As up his force the Tempest brings,
'Twere sweet, ere yet his terrors rave,
To sit upon the Wizard's grave;
That Wizard-Priest's, whose bones are thrust
From company of holy dust;
On which no sunbeam ever shines—
(So superstition's creed divines)

Thence view the lake, with sullen roar,
Heave her broad billows to the shore ;
And mark the wild swans mount the gale,
Spread wide through mist their snowy sail,
And ever stoop again, to lave
Their bosoms on the surging wave :
Then, when, against the driving hail,
No longer might my plaid avail,
Back to my lonely home retire,
And light my lamp, and trim my fire ;
There ponder o'er some mystic lay,
Till the wild tale had all its sway,
And, in the bittern's distant shriek,
I heard unearthly voices speak,
And thought the Wizard Priest was come,
To claim again his ancient home !
And bade my busy fancy range,
To frame him fitting shape and strange,
Till from the task my brow I clear'd,
And smiled to think that I had fear'd.

But chief, 'twere sweet to think such life,
(Though but escape from fortune's strife,)
Something most matchless good, and wise,
A great and grateful sacrifice ;
And deem each hour, to musing given,
A step upon the road to heaven.

Yet him, whose heart is ill at ease,
Such peaceful solitudes displease :

He loves to drown his bosom's jar
Amid the elemental war :
And my black Palmer's choice had been
Some ruder and more savage scene,
Like that which frowns round dark Loch-skene.
There eagles scream from isle to shore ;
Down all the rocks the torrents roar ;
O'er the black waves incessant driven,
Dark mists infect the summer heaven ;
Through the rude barriers of the lake,
Away its hurrying waters break,
Faster and whiter dash and curl,
Till down yon dark abyss they hurl.
Rises the fog-smoke white as snow,
Thunders the viewless stream below,
Diving, as if condemned to lave
Some demon's subterranean cave,
Who, prisoned by enchanter's spell,
Shakes the dark rock with groan and yell.
And well that Palmer's form and mien
Had suited with the stormy scene,
Just on the edge, straining his ken
To view the bottom of the den,
Where, deep, deep down, and far within,
Toils with the rocks the roaring linn ;
Then, issuing forth one foamy wave,
And wheeling round the Giant's Grave,
White as the snowy charger's tail,
Drives down the pass of Moffatdale.

WILLIAM LAIDLAW.

———◆———

WILLIAM LAIDLAW was born at Blackhouse, on the Douglas Burn, near St. Mary's Loch, November 19, 1780. He was sprung of a good stock. His father, James Laidlaw, was a man of quite exceptional intelligence and ability. William was the eldest of three sons, and seems to have received an excellent education. He was the intimate and life-long friend of James Hogg, who was for ten years a shepherd in Blackhouse. Laidlaw was one of the first to recognise the "Shepherd's" poetical genius, and he gave him much encouragement in the prosecution of his literary labours. Sir Walter Scott met him in 1801, when he was going from house to house all over the Border country collecting materials for his *Minstrelsy*, and from the first he seems to have entertained a strong liking for him, He began life by renting a farm on the Traquair estate, afterwards going to one at Liberton, near Edinburgh; but, like Hogg, he was not successful as a farmer. In 1817 he became steward to Sir Walter at Abbotsford, and here he remained for several years, securing the warm esteem of his employer, whom he in turn almost worshipped. Part of his time was spent in literary work, the fruits of which were mainly contributed to the *Edinburgh*

L 2

Annual Register.   The terrible crisis which occurred in Sir
Walter's financial affairs necessitated his leaving Abbotsford
for a short period.   He returned, however, in 1830, and
continued in his former position till Scott's death in 1832.
After this he went to Ross-shire as factor to Sir Charles
Lockart Ross, of Balnagowan, but his health failing he retired
and went to reside with his brother near Dingwall, where he
died May 18, 1845, aged 65.

Besides his well known and highly popular song, "Lucy's
Flittin'," which was first published in Hogg's *Forest Minstrel*
in 1810, Laidlaw was the author of the sweet and simple songs,
"Her Bonnie Black E'e" and "Alake for the Lassie."   He
also wrote on "Scottish Superstitions" to the *Edinburgh
Magazine;* contributed several articles to the *Encyclopædia;* and
was the author of a geological description of his native county.
Had he given himself to literature he might have become
eminent, as he had intellectual powers of a high and rare order;
but he does not seem to have been moved by any powerful
literary ambition.   "Lucy's Flittin'" will certainly prove the
most lasting memorial of his literary genius.   The last
verse of the song is from the pen of the "Ettrick Shepherd."
It is generally understood that he is the "Jamie"—"sae
dowie and cheerless,"—and that the incident so pathetically
described is based on fact.

Some difficulty has been experienced in fixing the locality of
the scene.   The residents on the banks of the Quair are of
opinion that "The Glen," now the magnificent mansion of

Sir Charles Tennant, Bart., is the place referred to. On the other hand the writer has interviewed a number of Laidlaw's relatives—(some of them knew the poet intimately) —and also several old people in the district, and the only opinion he has ever elicited is that " the glen " alluded to in the song is the one through which the Douglas Burn meanders to the Yarrow. This view finds confirmation in the poem itself. In the first edition of Hogg's *Forest Minstrel* the line runs thus :—

" And Lucy had served *i' the glen* a' the simmer."

The italics are ours, but the fact that " glen " is not printed with a capital " G " is strong evidence that Laidlaw was not thinking of the *house* of that name. The expression applies admirably to the situation of Blackhouse, and until much stronger evidence is forthcoming than has yet been produced, every reader of Laidlaw's poem will be more than justified in fixing the scene of the incident in the glen of the Douglas Burn.

LUCY'S FLITTIN'.

'Twas when the wan leaf frae the birk tree was fa'in',
    And Martinmas dowie had wound up the year,
That Lucy row'd up her wee kist, wi' her a' in,
    And left her auld master and neebours sae dear.

For Lucy had served i' the glen a' the simmer;
  She cam' there afore the flow'r bloom'd on the pea;
An orphan was she, an' they had been gude till her,
  Sure that was the thing brocht the tear in her e'e.

She gaed by the stable where Jamie was stan'in';
  Richt sair was his kind heart the flittin' to see.
"Fare ye weel, Lucy," quo' Jamie, and ran in,
  The gatherin' tears trickled fast frae his e'e.
As doun the burnside she gaed slow wi' her flittin',
  "Fare ye weel, Lucy," was ilka bird's sang.
She heard the craw sayin't, high on the tree sittin',
  And Robin was chirpin't the brown leaves amang.

"Oh! what is't that pits my puir heart in a flutter?
  An' what gars the tear come sae fast to my e'e?
If I wasna ettled to be ony better,
  Then what gars me wish ony better to be?
I'm just like a lammie that loses its mither;
  Nae mither or friend the puir lammie can see;
I fear I hae left my bit heart a' thegither,
  Nae wonder the tear fa's sae fast frae my e'e.

"Wi' the rest o' my claes I hae row'd up the ribbon,
  The bonny blue ribbon that Jamie ga'e me;
Yestreen, when he ga'e me't and saw I was sabbin',
  I'll never forget the wae blink o' his e'e.
Though now he said naething but "Fare ye weel, Lucy!"
  It made me I neither could speak, hear, nor see;
He couldna say mair, but just "Fare ye weel, Lucy!"
  Yet that I will mind till the day that I dee.

"The lamb likes the gowan wi' dew when its droukit;
   The hare likes the brake, and the braird on the lee;
But Lucy likes Jamie;"—she turned an' she lookit,
   She thocht the dear place she wad never mair see.
Ah! weel may young Jamie gang dowie an' cheerless!
   And weel may he greet on the bank o' the burn!
For bonny sweet Lucy, sae gentle an' peerless,
   Lies cauld in her grave, and will never return.

JOHN WILSON

JOHN WILSON, better known as *Christopher North*, was born in Paisley—a town which has been honoured as the birth-place of many illustrious men—on the 18th May, 1785. He began life with almost every advantage that can fall to the lot of any son of Adam. His father was a man of intelligence and culture, and blessed with no mean share of this world's goods. His mother had gentle blood in her veins; was lineally descended by the female side from the great Marquis of Montrose, a fact which may have had something to do both with Wilson's physical and mental characteristics. In his childish years, we are told, he was as beautiful and animated a creature as ever played in the sunshine. We are not surprised to learn that his passion for sports, especially for angling, was developed at an early period. He was not more than three years of age when he had the infinite and never-to-be-forgotten satisfaction of landing his first trout! This incident produced a deep impression on his mind, and created within him a passion for the gentle craft, which was extinguished only with life. But in his childhood he was fond of preaching as well as fishing, and was wont to amuse the family by delivering an impassioned discourse on the text—"There was a fish, and a deil o' a fish, and it was ill to its young anes." Like the "Beadle" in *Dean Ramsay*, he had no difficulty in drawing an inference. He had much to say about parents that were kind to their children, and others that were the reverse, and, as may be imagined, the bad ones were somewhat severely dealt with by this budding professor of Moral Philosophy. In his case the principle that "the boy is father to the man" was abundantly illustrated, for throughout life his passion for sport was equalled only by his love of oratory. Either in the ring or the rostrum he had but few superiors.

He began his education under a Mr Peddie, who was then teacher of the English school in Paisley, but when quite young he was placed under the tutorial supervision of the minister in the neighbouring parish of Mearns, Dr M'Latchie, who seems to have given his pupils sound instruction, combined with ample freedom to indulge in all manner of out-of-door pastimes. Many a memorable day was spent by the burn sides, or scouring the heathy uplands, thus laying up, if not impressions of an intellectual kind, at least a store of good health against the demands of later life. In 1797, at the early age of fourteen, Wilson matriculated as a student in Glasgow University, and had the good fortune to be boarded with Professor Jardine, a wise, genial, scholarly man, who took a lively interest in his welfare. He does not seem to have been greatly burdened by the ordinary routine of class work. Rarely indeed was it necessary for him to burn the midnight oil, but this was doubtless due in great part to his wonderful capacity for mastering a subject long before others of less ready wit had begun to realise its bearings. His philosophical genius asserted itself in the logic class, where he easily out-distanced all competitors. In some cases great minds ripen slowly, but it was not so in his. The seed time gave every promise of an abundant harvest—a prophecy which was amply fulfilled. It is interesting to note that Wilson was one of the first in this country to recognise the genius of Wordsworth, and when a student in Glasgow, wrote a long letter to the poet expressing his admiration. This letter, which is one of the earliest productions of his pen, gives indication of a keen and subtle intellect, and of a warm and generous heart.

In 1803 he entered as a gentleman commoner of Magdalen College, Oxford. He was now free to choose his own path in life, and to one situated as he was, with plenty of money at his command, and thus freed from the necessity of exerting himself in order to gain a material end,—there was a strong temptation to fall into a life either of idleness, or, worse still, of dissipation. That he did not lead an idle life is evident from the fact that he passed the final examination for his degree with great distinction; and in regard to his habits otherwise, they were doubtless much akin to those of the average Oxonian of that period. He had a liking for the inns where the coaches stopped, and probably spent more time in such places than he should have done.

His physical vigour at this period, as, indeed, throughout life, was extraordinary. He was close on six feet in height; broad-shouldered, deep chested, strong limbed—a man not to be trifled with. His pugilistic and pedestrian exploits filled the minds of his friends and fellow-students with a feeling of amazement. De Quincey says :—" There was no man who had any talents, real or fancied, for thumping or being thumped, but he had experienced some *preeing* of his merits from John Wilson. All other pretensions to the gymnastic arts he took a pride in humbling or in honouring, but chiefly his examinations fell upon pugilism,—and not a man who could 'give' or 'take' but waited to have punished, or been punished, by *Wilson of Mallens.*" The following anecdote, which, we are assured, has the merit of being true, fully bears out De Quincey's statement.

"Meeting one day with a rough and unruly wayfarer, who showed inclination to pick a quarrel concerning right of passage across a certain bridge, the fellow obstructed the way, and making himself decidedly obnoxious, Wilson lost all patience and offered to fight him. The man made no objection to the proposal, but replied that he had better not fight with *him*, as he was so and so, mentioning the name of a (then not unknown) pugilist. This statement, as may be supposed, had no effect in damping the belligerent intentions of the Oxonian; he knew his own strength, and his skill too. In one moment off went his coat, and he set to on his antagonist in splendid style. The astonished and *punished* rival, on recovering from his blows and surprise, accosted him thus: 'You can only be one of the two; you are either Jack Wilson or the devil.'" Many incidents of a similar nature might be recorded, as Wilson's interest in such pugilistic encounters was life-long. But his pedestrian feats at this period are, perhaps, even more remarkable than his pugilistic skill. On one occasion, when in London, he happened to have an encounter on the street with a fellow who had insulted him, and having punished him somewhat severely, he thought he had better get out of the way. Though the evening was well advanced, he started to walk to Oxford, a distance of sixty miles, where he arrived in the early morning!

Having completed his studies at Oxford, he retired to Elleray, a small estate he had purchased in Westmoreland, on Lake Windermere. The situation is one of the finest in that charming country, commanding a view of the lake from one extremity to the other, with its deeply indented and richly wooded shores, and emerald islands "chased in gold." Here he enjoyed the friendship of Wordsworth, De Quincey, (who was then residing in the neighbourhood), and Hartley Coleridge, a man of rare genius; but strangely deficient in self control. Though without a profession, or calling of any kind, he was not idle, nor did time hang heavy on his hands. He now began in earnest to write poetry. Long anterior to this he had been conscious of the divine afflatus, but hitherto his thoughts had been otherwise engaged. The opportunity, however, had come, and he was ready to embrace it. *The Isle of Palms* was the first garnered fruit of his poetical genius. The book was favourably received, and at once established the reputation of its author. But troublous times were at hand. His literary activity was destined to be stimulated, as in the case of Sir Walter Scott, by a painful, and, what would have been to many, an overwhelming disaster. An uncle in whom he seems to have reposed implicit confidence, proved unfaithful,—acted, indeed, the part of the unjust steward,—and in a moment Wilson was left almost penniless. It was a terrible blow, more especially as he had only a short time before been married to an amiable and accomplished lady, and had thus become involved in the cares of a household and family. Though his equanimity was thus rudely disturbed, he did not yield to the spirit of despair. He knew that he could easily make a way for himself in the world, and he at once began to lay his plans. He resolved to study for the bar; and

in course of time we find him in Edinburgh doing his utmost
to secure the necessary qualifications.   Ere long he is pacing
the Hall of Parliament House, wigged and gowned—a full-
blown advocate.   Had he applied himself, it is highly probable
that he would have risen to a distinguished position ; but the
intricacies and minutiæ of the law were but little to his liking.
He occasionally got cases, but when he found them on his table
he used to say that "he did not know what the devil to do with
them."

It was about this time (1815) that he made his first pilgrimage
to the " Dowie Dens o' Yarrow."   He walked from Edinburgh
to Peebles on a Saturday in the month of June, arriving there,
he tells us, a perfect *lameter*, his shoes having " peeled his
timbers."   He thus describes his further progress :—" On
Monday morning at six o'clock (miraculous !) I uprose from
the couch of slumber, and walked along the Tweed to
Traquair Knowe (Mr Laidlaw's).   There I fished, and stayed
all morning, the place being very beautiful.   Mr Laidlaw is
married, an insectologist and poet, and farmer and agriculturist.
On Tuesday morning I walked to Hogg's, a distance of about
eight miles, fishing as I went, and surprised him in his cottage
bottling whisky.   He is well and dressed pastorally.   His
house is not habitable, but the situation is good and may
become pretty.   There being no beds in his domicile, we last
night came here, a farmer's house about a quarter of a mile
from him, where I have been treated most kindly and hospi-
tably.   The house and entertainment something *a la Wastdale*,

but much superior. I have risen at seven o'clock, and am
preparing to take a complete day's fishing among the streams
near St. Mary's Loch." "On one of these fishing excursions,"
we are told, "he had proceeded from St. Mary's Loch to
Peebles, where he could not at first get admittance to the inn,
as it was fully occupied by a party of country gentlemen, met
together on some county business. On sending in his name,
however, he was immediately asked to join them at dinner. It
is needless to say that, under his spell, the fun grew fast and
furious. No one thought of moving. Supper was proposed,
and as nothing eatable was to be had in the house, Wilson
asked the company if they liked trouts, and forthwith produced
the result of his day's amusement from basket, bag, and pocket,
in such numbers that the table was soon literally covered. As
the Shepherd afterwards said :—' Your creel was fu'—your
shooting bag fu'—your jacket-pouches fu'—the pouches o'
your verra breeks fu'—half-a-dozen wee anes in your waistcoat,
no to forget them in the crown o' your hat,—and, last o' a,
when there was nae place to stow awa' ony mair, a willow wand
through the gills o' some great big anes.'" The angler's-silent
trade was a ruling passion with Wilson. His enthusiasm never
flagged. In order to enjoy his favourite pastime, he would
walk sometimes fifty or sixty miles to some stream or loch
among the hills. On such occasions he always felt that a good
day's sport more than compensated him for all the discomforts
of the journey. "In he used to gang," the Shepherd says,
" out, out, out, and ever sae far out frae the point o' a

promontory, sinking aye further and further doon, first to the
waistband o' his breeks, then up to the middle button o' his
waistcoat, then to the verra briest, then to the oxters, then to the
neck, and then to the verra chin o' him, sae that ye wunnered
how he could fling the flee; till, last o' a', he would plump
richt oot o' sicht, till the Highlander on Ben Cruachan thocht
him drooned. No he, indeed; sae he takes to the sooming,
and strikes awa' wi' ae arm, for the tither had haud o' the rod;
and could ye believ't, though its as true as Scripture, fishing a'
the time, that no a moment o' the cloudy day micht be lost;
ettles at an island a quarter o' a mile aff, wi' trees, and an auld
ruin o' a religious house, wherein beads used to be counted,
and wafers eaten, and mass uttered hundreds o' years ago; and
getting footing on the yellow sand or green sward, he but gies
himself a shake, and ere the sun looks out o' the clud, has
hyucket a four-pounder, whom, in four miuutes (for its a
multiplying pirn the cretur uses), he lands gasping through the
the giant gills, and glittering wi' a thousand spots, streaks,
and stars, on the shore."

The love of fishing first brought Wilson to Yarrow, but
soon the valley, with its quiet beauty and romantic associations,
cast its spell over his genius, as in so many other cases, and
held him a willing captive to its charms. He became a warm
friend, and an ardent admirer of the Ettrick Shepherd, and
many a jovial night he spent in his society at Altrive and
Mount Benger, when Hogg would doubtless sing of his own,
and with that weird "lilt," suggestive of mountain solitude, by

which his vocal muse was characterised. And the fiddle, too, would often be in requisition, and when the floor was cleared for a reel, the lads and lassies with one accord would join in the merry dance, led on by the buoyant Professor, who was an adept in everything pertaining to the calisthenic art.

But for everything there is a time and a season. Such hours of innocent gaiety were followed by days of quiet wandering by mountain, moor, and stream, when the mind had time to reflect on the great problems of nature and life, and to drink in the inspiration which breathes upon the soul through the manifold forms of beauty with which the Creator has adorned the world. Then what glorious conversations of an evening as the two poets sat by the fire long after the other members of the household had gone to rest. It was then he studied the ways of the Shepherd, became familiar with his modes of thought and feeling, and was thus able to depict him with inimitable humour in the *Noctes Ambrosianæ*. That Wilson loved Yarrow—was fascinated by it—we cannot doubt; but he has not given such full expression to this feeling in his poetry as might have been expected. There are many passages in the *Noctes* which indicate clearly enough his interest in the Vale, and keen appreciation of its natural beauty and historic charms; but his poems are all but silent on this theme. The reason of this is not far to seek. After he went to Edinburgh he found his hands more than full. His contributions to *Blackwood* alone were enough to keep an ordinary man busy; but in addition to this he filled the Chair of Moral Philosophy in the University—an office which necessarily entailed large demands on his time and energies.

Mrs Gordon has given a delightful account of a visit which Wilson paid to Tibbie Shiel's. "True to his love for spring," she says, " he had selected that season for an excursion to the pastoral vales of Yarrow and Ettrick, where glittering rivers,

'Winding through the pomp of cultivated nature,'

attracted more than one poet's admiration, for if Wordsworth sang in verse, Wilson uttered in prose how ' in spirit all streams are one that flow through the Forest. Ettrick and Yarrow come rushing into each other's arms aboon the haughs o' Selkirk, and then flow Tweed-blent to the sea.' In the month of May he sent an invitation to his students resident in the south of Scotland, to meet him at 'Tibbie Shiel's,' where they were to wander a day with him, 'to enjoy the first gentle embrace of spring in some solitary spot.' Where could it have been better selected than at St. Mary's Loch? It was said that the meeting was one of unspeakable delight; the hills were adorned with the freshest green, and the calm quiet lake reflected the surrounding verdure in its deep waters, and they beheld

> 'The swan on still St. Mary's Lake,
> Float double, swan and shadow.'

The Professor spoke of the love of nature, and his words impressed them all, and of the poet of Altrive, 'our own Shepherd,' dear to all the rills that issue, in thousands, from their own recesses among the braes; for when a poet walks through regions his genius has sung, all nature does him homage, from cloud to clod—from the sky to green earth—all living creatures therein included, from eagle to the mole. James knows this, and is happy among the hills. And was that little company assembled by the 'dowie holms' not happy too? Wilson was in his brightest mood; no one was overlooked; joyously and pleasantly passed the day; and before evening laid its westering shadows into gloaming, he called his students around him, and, rising up, 'he shook his wild locks among them, blessed them, called them his children,' and bade them adieu."

In the year 1854 John Wilson was gathered to his fathers. He was deeply and sincerely mourned by a large circle of friends and admirers. A splendid statue was erected to his memory in Princes Street Gardens, Edinburgh, which will long preserve the leonine aspect of a face at once massive and refined. But while his name and fame are most intimately associated with the city of his adoption, yet Yarrow claims him as one of her warmest admirers, and as long as Tibbie Shiel's, Mount Benger, and Altrive are suggestive of associations dear to the Scottish muse, the memory of John Wilson will be fragrant.

It may be said that Wilson has no claim to be ranked among the poets of Yarrow. He has written many poems, but with one exception—and in this case the allusion is indefinite—he has never embalmed in verse the romance of the valley. The force of this objection must be frankly admitted, yet many of his descriptions in the *Noctes* may be regarded as prose poems, and these, too, of a high order. In the following description of a snow storm in Yarrow, we have an admirable illustration of what is meant :—

" *Tickler*—' O, my dear James, conversation is at a very low ebb in this world !'

" *Shepherd*—' I've often thought and felt that at parties where ane micht hae expeckit better things. First o' a' comes the wather—no a bad toppic, but ane that town's folks ken naething about. Wather ! my faith, had ye been but in Yarrow last Thursday.'

"*Tickler*—'What was the matter, James, last Thursday in Yarrow?'

"*Shepherd*—'I'se tell you, and judge for yoursel'. At four in the morning it was that hard frost that the dubs were bearin', and the midden was as hard as a rickle o' stanes. We couldna plant the powtatoes. But the lift was clear. Between eight and nine, a snaw storm came down frae the mountains about Lochskeen, noo a whirl, and noo a blash, till the grun' was whitey-blue, wi' a sliddery sort o' sleet, and the Yarrow began to roar wi' the melted broo, alang its frost-bound borders, and aneath its banks, a' hanging wi' icicles, nane o' them thinner than my twa arms. Weel, then, about eleven it began to rain, for the wund had shifted—and afore dinner-time, it was an even-down pour. It fell lown about sax, and the air grew close and sultry to a degree that was fearsome. Wha wud hae expeckit a thunder storm on the eve o' sic a day? But the heavens in the thundery airt were like a dungeon, and I saw the lightning playing like meteors athwart the blackness, long before ony growl was in the gloom. Then, a' at ance, like a waukened lion, the thunder rose up in his den, and shaking his mane o' brindled clouds, broke out with sic a roar that the very sun shuddered in eclipse, and the grews and collies that happened to be sittin' beside me on a bit knowe, gaed whinin' into the house wi' their tails atween their legs, just venturin' a halflin glance to the howlin' heavens noo a' in lowe, for the fire was strong and fierce in electrical matter, and at intervals the illuminated mountains seemed to vomit out conflagration like verra volcanoes.

'Afore sunset, heaven and earth, like lovers after a quarrel, lay embraced in each other's smile!'

" *North*—' Beautiful! Beautiful! Beautiful!'

" *Tickler*—' Oh! James. James, James!'

" *Shepherd*—'The lambs began their races on the lea, and the thrush o' Eltrive (there is but a single pair in the vale aboon the Kirk) awoke his hymn in the hill-silence. It was mair like a mornin' than evenin' twilight, and a' the day's hurly-burly had passed awa' into the uncertainty o' a last week's dream.'

" *North*—' Proof positive that, from the lips of a man of genius, even the weather'—

" *Shepherd*—' I could speak for hours, days, months, and years, about the wather without e'er becoming tiresome. O man, a cawm!'

" *North*—' On shore, or at sea?'

" *Shepherd*—' Either. I'm wrapped up in my plaid, and lyin' a' my length on a bit green platform, fit for the fairies' feet, wi' a craig hangin' ower me a thousand feet high, yet bright and balmy a' the way up wi' flowers and briars, and broom and birks, and mosses maist beautifu' to behold, wi' half-shut ee, and through aneath ane's arm, guardin' the face frae the cloudless sunshine!'

" *North*—' A rivulet leaping from the rock.'

" *Shepherd*—' No, Mr North, no loupin; for it seems as if it were nature's ain Sabbath, and the verra waters were at rest.

Look down upon the vale profound, and the stream is without motion! No doubt, if you were walking along the bank, it would be murmuring with your feet. But here—here up among the hills, we can imagine it asleep, even like the well within the reach of my staff!'

.   .   .   .

'Perhaps a bit bonny butterfly is resting, wi' faulded wings, on a gowan no a yard frae your cheek; and noo, waukening out o' a simmer dream, floats awa in its wavering beauty, but as if unwilling to leave its place of mid-day sleep, comin' back and back, and roun' and roun', on this side and that side, and ettlin', in its capricious happiness, to fasten again on some bright floweret, till the same breath o' wund that lifts up your hair sae refreshingly catches the airy voyager, and wafts her away into some other nook of her ephemeral paradise.'

"*Tickler*—'I did not know that butterflies inhabited the region of snow.'

"*Shepherd*—'Ay, and mony million moths; some o' as lovely green as the leaf of the moss-rose; and ithers bright as the blush with which she salutes the early dawn; some yellow as the long steady streaks that lie below the sun at set, and ithers blue as the sky before his orb has westered. Spotted, too, are all the glorious creatures' wings—say, rather, starred wi' constellations! Yet, O, sirs, they are but creatures o' a day!'

"*North*—'Go on with the calm, James—the calm!'

"*Shepherd*—'Gin a pile o' grass straughtens itself in silence,

you hear it distinctly. I'm thinking that was the noise o' a
beetle gaun to pay a visit to a freen on the ither side o' that
mossy stane. The melting dew quakes! Ay, sing awa', my
bonny bee, maist industrious o' God's creatures! Dear me, the
heat is ower muckle for him; and he burrows himsel' in amang
a tuft o' grass, like a beetle panting! and noo invisible a' but
the yellow doup o' him. I too feel drowsy, and will go to sleep
among the mountain solitude.'

" *North*—' Not with such a show of clouds.'

" *Shepherd*—' No! not with such a show of clouds. A
congregation of a million might worship in that Cathedral.
What a dome! And is not that flight o' steps magnificent?
My imagination sees a crowd of white-robed spirits ascending
to the inner shrine of the temple. Hark! a bell tolls! Yonder
it is, swinging to and fro, half-minute time, in its tower of
clouds. The great air organ 'gins to blow its pealing anthem—
and the overcharged spirit falling from its vision, sees nothing
but the pageantry of earth's common vapours—that ere long
will melt in showers, or be wafted away in darker masses over
the distance of the sea. Of what better stuff, O, Mr North, are
made all our waking dreams?' "

HENRY SCOTT RIDDLE.

H ENRY SCOTT RIDDLE was born at Sorbie, in the vale of Ewes, a few miles from Langholm, Dumfriesshire, in September 23, 1798. His father, who was a man of superior intelligence, followed the occupation of shepherd. At an early age Henry was hired, during the summer months, to herd a neighbour's cows, and in winter he was sent to the parish school, where he received an excellent elementary training. He was not in his earlier years particularly enamoured of books, owing, doubtless, to some extent, to the fact that he was not kept regularly at school; but as he grew up he began to realise the importance of study, and as a young man he applied himself enthusiastically to the task of self-improvement. He read much and widely on all subjects. His environment was also in the highest degree favourable to the development of his poetical tastes. He was for a period of two years a shepherd on the farm of Deloraine, then in the parish of Yarrow, now belonging to the *Quoad Civilia* parish of Kirkhope, tenanted by a Mr Scott, the grandfather of the present lessee. His father was for many years in Mr Scott's employment, and Henry was named after him. Report bears that he

was a skilful and eminently trustworthy shepherd, who never
went to the hill without a book of some kind or other hid under
the folds of his plaid. But his passion for books does not
seem to have interfered with the proper discharge of his onerous
duties.   Here, on the green hills lying along the banks of the
Ettrick, as he tended his gentle flock, he read the masterpieces
of English literature, and stored his mind with ideas and facts
which, in after years, he employed to such excellent purpose.
Referring to this interesting and important period of his life,
he says :—

> " My early years were pass'd far on
> The hills of Ettrick wild and lone ;
> Through summer sheen and winter shade,
> Tending the flocks that o'er them stray'd.
> In bold enthusiastic glee
> I sung rude strains of minstrelsy,
> Which, mingling with, died o'er the dale,
> Unheeded as the plover's wail.
> Oft where the waving rushes shed
> A shelter frail around my head,
> Weening, though not through hopes of fame,
> To fix on these more lasting claim,
> I'd there secure in rustic scroll
> The wayward fancies of the soul.
> Even where yon lofty rocks arise,
> Hoar as the clouds in wintry skies,
> Wrapp'd in the plaid, and dern'd beneath
> The colder cone of drifted wreath.
> I noted them afar from ken,
> Till ink would freeze upon the pen ;
> So deep the spell which bound the heart
> Unto the bard's undying art—
> So rapt the charm that still beguiled
> The minstrel of the mountains wild."

After leaving Deloraine he went to Todrig, a farm on
the River Ale, near Hawick. Here he made the acquaint-
ance of William Knox, the author of "The Lonely Hearth,"
a man whose genius and intellectual ability were warmly

recognised by Professor Wilson and Sir Walter Scott. "While here," he says, "my whole leisure time was employed in writing. I composed while walking and looking the hill. I also wrote down among the wilds. I yet remember, as in a dream of poetry itself, how blessedly bright and beautiful exceedingly were these wilds themselves early in summer mornings, or when the white mists filled up the glens below, and left the summits of the mountains near and far away as sight could travel, green, calm, and serene as an eternity."

His father died, leaving him a small sum of money, and he now determined to apply himself to study, with a view to entering the ministry. He went to a school in Biggar, where he acquired the rudiments of classical learning, and in due time he enrolled himself as a student in the University of Edinburgh. His career was not brilliant. He entered college at an age when most other students are leaving, and consequently it was hardly to be expected that he should carry off many prizes. He attracted the attention, however, of more than one professor. Dunbar, the famous lexicographer, was delighted with the way in which he translated one of the Odes of Anacreon—his skill in versification standing him in good stead. He was also a favourite with Professor Wilson, who took a kindly interest in his studies, and often invited him to spend an evening at his house.

Shortly after completing his theological curriculum, he was appointed by the Duke of Buccleuch to the newly formed parish of Teviothead. His stipend was very small. Like

another famous parson, it might also be said of him that " he
was passing rich on forty pounds a year." His actual stipend
was £52 per annum, but then he had no manse, and con-
sequently was under the necessity of renting a house. He lived
for some years in the farm-house of Flex, nine miles distant
from the church, and as he could not afford to keep a horse, he
had to walk eighteen miles every Sunday, so that, all things
considered, his office was no sinecure. An incident which
occurred shortly before he went to live in the manse which the
Duke ultimately erected for the minister of the parish, was
the occasion of the composition of that beautiful lyric,
"The Emigrant's Wish." Returning home from preaching one
Sunday afternoon, wet and weary, Mrs Riddle, doubtless
anticipating the comforts of the new home, exclaimed, "Ah!
Henry, I wish we were hame to our ain folk."

His ministry in this rural parish was much appreciated by all
classes; but in 1841, nine years after his ordination, he was
laid aside from active duty by a severe nervous malady, from
which he was long in recovering. It was not thought advisable
that he should resume the duties of the pastorate, but the Duke,
with that large-hearted generosity so characteristic of the house
of Buccleuch, gave him the manse during his life-time, along
with a small annuity, and a few acres of ground.

Riddle was a voluminous author. When a student he com-
posed many songs for the *Irish Minstrel* and *Select Melodies*
of R. A. Smith, and for the original *National Melodies* of
Peter M‘Leod. In 1841 he published his *Songs of the Ark, and*

other Poems, followed in 1844 by a prose work, entitled: *The Christian Politician; or, the Right Way of Thinking.* In 1847 another volume of poetry appeared, entitled *Poems, Songs, and Miscellaneous Pieces.* He also published a book on *Store Farming in the South of Scotland.*

Many of his songs have attained a wide and well-deserved popularity. "The Crook and Plaid," "The Emigrant's Wish," and "Scotland Yet," are often sung, and will long retain a high place among the best and most popular songs in the language. His "Dowie Dens o' Yarrow" is not one of his most successfu efforts, but he has succeeded in catching to some extent the spirit of the old ballads. This song, however, deserves a place here not merely on the ground of its intrinsic merit, but because we may almost claim Henry Scott Riddle as a native of the Vale. His father lived for many years in Yarrow, and, as we have already noticed, Henry was also for a time resident in the district.

THE DOWIE DENS O' YARROW.

Oh, sister, there are midnight dreams
    That pass not with the morning,
Then ask not why my reason swims
    In a brain sae wildly burning;
And ask not why I fancy how
    Yon wee birds sing wi' sorrow,
For bluid lies mingled with the dew
    In the dowie dens o' Yarrow.

My dream's wild light was not o' night,
   Nor o' the doolfu' morning,
Thrice on the stream was seen the gleam
   That seemed his sprite returning;
For sword-girt men came down the glen,
   An hour before the morrow,
And pierced the heart aye true to mine,
   In the dowie dens o' Yarrow.

Oh! there are red, red drops o' dew
   Upon the wild flower's blossom,
But they couldna cool my burning brow,
   And shall not stain my bosom;
But from the clouds o' yon dark sky
   A cold, cold shroud I'll borrow,
And long and deep shall be my sleep
   In the dowie dens o' Yarrow.

This from the bluid-died flower shall press
   By the heart o' him that lo'ed me;
And I'll steal frae his lips a long, long kiss,
   In the bower where oft he wooed me;
For my arm shall fold and my tresses shield
   The form o' my death-cold marrow,
When the breeze shall bring the raven's wing
   O'er the dowie dens o' Yarrow.

JOHN STUART BLACKIE.

THERE are few names more intimately associated with the life and literature of Scotland than that of John Stuart Blackie. For more than half a century his name has been a household word, and though now an octogenarian, it may be said that " his eye is not yet dim, neither is his natural strength abated." His literary activity is phenomenal. In his time he has played many parts—Poet, Preacher, Patriot, and Professor of Greek—and it is difficult to determine in which he appears to greatest advantage, as in every work to which he applies himself he seems as if to the manner born. Though intensely Scottish in his sympaties, he is none the less an enthusiastic cosmopolite, and feels almost as much at home in Athens, Rome, and Berlin, as in his own beloved Edinburgh.

He is one of the few distinguished Scotsmen born *furth* of Paisley! Glasgow claims him as one of her sons. Here he first saw the light on July 28, 1809. But his father, who was a banker, removed to Aberdeen when John was quite young— a circumstance not without important consequences. He entered Marischal College at the age of twelve, and under the distinguished guidance of Professor Melvin—a splendid scholar and thoroughly capable teacher — he acquired an intimate knowledge of Latin, being able to read not only the most difficult authors with facility, but to converse freely in the language of the Cæsars. He studied Divinity in Edinburgh with a view to entering the Church; but difficulties of a theological kind led him ultimately to abandon this idea. He went to the continent in 1829, and studied both at Göttingen and Berlin. He then went to Italy, where he remained for some months studying with much enthusiasm the language, literature, and archæology of the country. Returning to Edinburgh, he began studying for the bar, to which in course of time he was duly called. Not finding the intricacies of the law much to his liking, he gave himself heartily to literature, contributing numerous articles to the leading Magazines and Reviews. His first work of any importance was a translation of Goethe's *Faust*—a production which afforded ample evidence of his intimate and scholarly acquaintance with the German language. In 1841 he was appointed Professor of Humanity in Aberdeen. During the eleven years in which he held this appointment his literary activity was unabated. He published a translation of the dramas of *Æschylus*, which he dedicated to Chevalier Bunsen and Edward Gerhard, " the friends of his youth and the directors of his early studies."

In 1852 he was elected to the Chair of Greek in the University of Edinburgh, a position from which he retired after thirty years service.

His books are numerous. The following are a few of the more important :—*Lays and Legends of Ancient Greece, and other Poems* (1857); *Homer and the Iliad* (1866); *Lays of the Highlands and Islands* (1872); *Self-Culture* (1874); *Songs of Religion and Life* (1876); *The Language and Literature of the Highlands* (1877); *Life of Burns* (1888), &c., &c.

In 1889 Professor Blackie resided for three months in Yarrow, and, as might be expected, manifested a lively interest in the traditions and history of the Vale. The following poems were written during this period, and, apart from their general literary merits, they are deeply interesting on account of the local setting which the author has been careful to give them.

RENWICK AT RISKINHOPE.

At Tibbie Shiel's here let them dance
    And sing, I blame them not;
They came to play, e'en let them play,
But something in my heart to-day
Directs my steps—and I obey—
    To a more sacred spot.

But yesterday I passed, and saw
    At head of Moffat Water,
'Neath the sheer linn the darksome den
That hid the covenanting men
From the hot hunt, and hungry ken
    Of eyes that fed on slaughter.

N

And here again is holy ground ;
    Of Scotland's martyr band
Latest and best, the noble boy   ·
Who scorned the bribe that would alloy
The truth with lies, in God's employ
    Preached in this mountain land.

Mark well yon white house 'mid the trees ;
    There, chased from glen to glen
By bloodhounds of a despot race,
Young Renwick found a sheltering place,
With looks of love and deeds of grace
    From simple plaided ̣men.

Come, let us go !   So said, so done :
    We clomb the brae together,
O'er stock and stone and mossy ground,
And huge broad hills that hemmed us round,
With swathes of grass all rankly crowned,
    And tufts of shaggy heather.

Up we clomb, and down we slid,
    Sheer to a mountain brook ;
Where on a sloping grassy mound
The people sate, in circle round,
And pulpit free the brave youth found,
    To preach from holy book.

Mark well that stump, where once there grew
   A thorn, a goodly tree ;
Even there he stood, and 'gan to sing
A powerful psalm, on faithful wing,
Most like to David, shepherd-king,
   Ruddy and fair to see.

And there he preached, but not as some,
   With eyes chained to a paper ;
Nor like to who in full career
Through seas of pleasant fancies steer,
With sounding phrase that charms the ear,
   And floats away in vapour.

But like a marksman trained and tried,
   To wing no doubtful arrow,
Who knows his ground and knows his game,
And with a sure determined aim
Brings down the prey he dared to claim—
   So Renwick preached in Yarrow.

" Their right to rule from righteous God
   Right-hearted rulers borrow ;
But for this treacherous, murtherous race,"
'Twas thus he spake, " disowned from grace,
Who for the devil wield the mace,
   We own them not in Yarrow.

N 2

" Who make us puppets of their will,
    To wait in servile station,
Well pleased to dance as they may pipe,
And from our souls the image wipe
Of God, and stamp it with the type
    Of priestly domination.

" Not to uphold a Popish throne,
    By hoar St. Andrews' tower,
Did Hamilton, the noble youth,
Beard the proud priest that knew no truth,
And, swathed in flame, for gospel truth
    Uplift his voice with power.

" Not from a king to beg the right
    Of prayer, on bended knee,
Did stout John Knox from gospel store,
With bolt of thunder smite the door
Of Rome, and with pure Bible lore
    Made Scotland strong and free.

" Let servile souls with courtly lies
    A base indulgence borrow ;
But you and I, and all the clan,
That own the noble name of man,
Will serve our God, and fear no ban
    From Prince or Pope in Yarrow."

So preached the fair-faced boy, and knew
   His preaching meant a deed;
When in his ear the fierce halloo
Sounded of Clavers and his crew,
Who all God's people did pursue
   To death, with murtherous speed.

He wept his last farewell; then crossed
   The hills to Manorhead;
Thence down to where, with gentle sweep,
Tweed winds its waters slow and deep,
By lofty Neidpath's castled keep,
   With hasty foot he sped.

Nor there might rest; but on and on
   Through Fife, a weary way;
And backward thence with shifty skill,
And foot with travel faint, until
Beneath Dun Edin's castled hill,
   The hunters trapped their prey;

And dragged him where stern judges sate
   In deathful judgment hall;
Who plied him hard with legal phrase,
But sat and wondered with amaze,
While calmly he protests and prays,
   " May God forgive you all!

" No laws against free-fielded prayer
   In God's true book are found ;
God is my judge: to Popish James
I owe no cess: to own his claims
Let him find liege men on the Thames,
   Not here on Scottish ground!"

Thus he : and calmly took his doom,
   And with firm front denied ;
And to the crowded market place
Moved firmly with a steady pace,
And with a glory in his face,
   Received the rope and died.

A LAY OF ST. MARY'S LOCH.

If there be who love to cherish
   Pleasant thoughts in peaceful wise,
Far from smoke-enfolden cities,
   'Neath blue curtain of the skies ;

Far from rush of fretful people,
   Blinding dust and dinsome jar,
Cries of self-applauding hawkers,
   Restive steed and rattling car ;

Far from press of dreary labour,
   Whirling wheel and whizzing loom,
Clanking chain and swinging hammer,
   Crowded hall and heated room ;

From the loveless strife of parties,
  And from churchly rancour free—
Let him come to lone St. Mary's
  Grassy-mantled hills with me ;

Let him roam with foot unchartered,
  Up the cleugh and down the slope—
Where the burnie brawls and brattles,
  Where the pine tree shields the Hope.*

Let him pace the ground and ponder,
  Where the Scot stout-hearted grew ;
Ever strong to strike for freedom—
  Douglas, Murray, and Buccleuch.

When our kings were babes and lordlings,
  Fought with lordlings for the sway ;
Then the brave lords of the border
  Kept the English churls at bay.

In his land a king was Murray,
  Holding rule and giving law,
Where the Yarrow seeks the Ettrick
  By the woods of Hangingshaw.

Lord was he of mighty bowmen,
  Sharp to shoot as ere was seen ;
Belted for the strife, and clad in
  Livery of the Lincome green.

* A farm-house built on a sort of delta or opening at the bottom of the mountain streams.

Bold Buccleuch he hated Murray,
　　Keen to blame and proud to spurn ;
Called him thief and called him outlaw,
　　From his hold in Rankleburn.

But King James, who knew more wisely
　　What a Murray's strength might be,
Came with pomp from high Dunedin,
　　With five thousand men came he.

Crossed the Tweed, and to the Outlaw
　　As a king swears truly swore,
What broad lands he won from England,
　　He might hold for evermore.*

With such memories fan thy patriot
　　Fire, of men that saved fair Tweed
From the grasp of greedy Southrons,
　　By brave word and manly deed.

Or, if pity move thee rather,
　　Take a tale of dole and sorrow,
Hanging by the grim old arches
　　Of some ivied tower in Yarrow.

Come with me across the Wardlaw,
　　To the burn† that bears a name
Brothered with the Bruce in battle,
　　To redress the Scot from shame.

* See the ballad of the Outlaw Murray, p. 32.

† The Douglas Burn, which, rising in the heights of Blackhouse, on the borders of Peebleshire, flows into the north bank of the Yarrow, about 1½ miles from the eastern end of the loch.

Come with me, and where the pine tree
    Spreads its sheltering arms with might,
Note the grim keep whence the lover
    Bore his love in dead of night.

Bold Sir William, little recking
    Father's force or mother's wrath,
Bore the daughter of the Douglas
    Lightly o'er the mountain path.

On a milk-white steed he bore her,
    When, behold ! as swift as wind,
Seven stout brothers, with the father,
    Followed on his track behind.

And they drew their brands, and dealt him
    Sharply many a bleeding wound,
But he paid them back more sharply,
    Laid them breathless on the ground.

But who wrought such scaithful ending,
    He might not from scaith be free,
Pale and faint, with Lady Margaret
    To his mother's hall rode he.

" Make my bed, for I am weary,"
    To his mother dear said he,
"Let me sleep, and let, dear Lady
    Margaret sleep not far from me."

And he slept and knew no waking,
   And she slept and woke no more,
And many wept and none were glad
   On St. Mary's pebbly shore.

Weep for them, and pray that lovers
   Nevermore may reap such sorrow
As the Douglas maid from love
   Watered with heart's blood in Yarrow.

.   .   .   .

See yon white hut in the far end
   Which the wood scarce half reveals,
That's the dear loved haunt of Douglas,
   That's the shrine of Tibbie Shiels,

Kindly hostess of St. Mary,
   Blithe and bountiful, shrewd and good,
He who knows not Tibbie, knows not
   Scotland in her happiest mood.

Here the choicest sons of Scotland,
   With health and wit and fishing rods,
Spent 'neath Tibbie's kindly tendance,
   Nights and suppers of the gods.

Glorious John, high Priest of Maga,
   Planted here his summer tent,
Lashed the loch, and swept the waters
   On his finny hunt intent.

Loved not he with lust of gazing,
   Far to feed the wandering eye,
Down the Seine and up the Rhine stream,
   Ever under some new sky.

Myrtle groves and stately palm trees,
   Seek who will with lengthened tether,
His were cheaper joys and better
   'Mid birch bowers and blooming heather.

All the day he lashed the water,
   And at gentle eventide
Keenly ate with healthful hunger,
   What the good dame might provide.

Ate and drank with stout contentment,
   Like a schoolboy tired of play,
Not alone, but with him gathered,
   In a friendly loose array,

Spirits worthy of his mettle,
   Flinging shots of wit about,
Plashing in broad swirls of humour,
   Like a young and lusty trout.

Learned judge from smokeful Glasgow,*
   Tall and with a stately pace,
Wise to mingle weighty sentence,
   With a word of light winged grace.

* Sheriff Glassford Bell.

Stoddart, king of angling rhymers,
  Who as blithe as bird in May,
Singing, fished, and fishing sang,
  All the streams from Tweed to Spey.

Hogg, that gleaned with pious gleaning
  All the flowers of minstrel lore,
That bloomed in Ettrick and in Yarrow
  In the good old days of yore.

These with him and others with them,
  Whom a kindly wind there blew,
True to Nature, true to Scotland,
  And to sportive wisdom true.

There they sat and drank and sang,
  Jolly boys well matched together,
Scarcely may such chums be found
  Now in all our breadth of heather.

JOHN CAMPBELL SHAIRP.

———————•———————

JOHN CAMPBELL SHAIRP was born at Houston, Linlithgowshire, on the 30th July, 1819. He was a descendant of an old and well-known family, the property of Houston having been acquired by the Shairps as far back as the sixteenth century. His interest in Yarrow is not difficult to account for, apart altogether from the historical associations of the district. He was a lineal descendant of Mary Harden Scott, "The Flower of Yarrow." His great-grandmother, Anne Scott of Harden, was the eldest daughter of John Scott, whose great-grandfather, Sir Gideon Scott, of High Chester, was grand-son of "The Flower of Yarrow." She was a Scott of Dryhope, and her romantic wooing is referred to in Shairp's poem, "Three Friends in Yarrow." "His maternal ancestry had a great interest for Shairp, and an inheritance of good, reaching from a distant past, was probably an influential element in the moulding of his character." His education was carried on at first under a tutor, but in course of time he was sent to the Edinburgh Academy, where he was fully equipped for entering College, which he did in 1836. He elected to study in Glasgow, and was boarded with the Rev. Dr. Macleod, father of the late gifted Dr. Norman Macleod, minister of the Barony, who became one of Shairp's most intimate friends. In 1840 he gained the Snell

Exhibition, and went to Oxford, where he had a highly respectable career, though not so brilliant as might have been anticipated, considering his many advantages, and the unflagging industry by which his student life was characterised. He thought at one time of entering the ministry of the Episcopal Church, but this idea he ultimately abandoned. He was appointed to a mastership in Rugby, under Tait, late Archbishop of Canterbury, who succeeded Arnold, and was doing his utmost to maintain the reputation which the school had attained under his distinguished predecessor. In Shairp he found an able and enthusiastic coadjutor. He entered heartily into the work, and became a great favourite both with the pupils and the numerous body of his fellow teachers. But the intellectual atmosphere of England was not a congenial one. He was intensely Scottish in all his sympathies, and yearned to return to "the land of the mountain and the flood." He was much gratified when he was appointed to the Professorship of Humanity in St. Andrew's, though the salary attached to this office was barely adequate to the most ordinary requirements. In this capacity he won the affectionate admiration of all his students—kindness and urbanity being always marked features of his character. In due time he was appointed to the Principalship, an office which he filled with credit to himself, and advantage to the University.

As already indicated, Shairp had an ancestral connection with the vale of Yarrow; and this, combined with his passionate fondness for piscatorial pursuits, may have induced him to visit the district at an early period of life. When he was only nineteen years of age he made a pilgrimage to St. Mary's Loch, and Tibbie Shiel's, and it is an interesting fact that his first published poem was inspired by the scenery and associations of this romantic region. He called it "A Remembrance of Two Days spent among the Braes of Yarrow, from the evening of Tuesday, the 25th, till the forenoon of Thursday, the 27th September, 1838."

In the year 1856 Professor Veitch—whose name is a household word all over the Border country—met him, and has recorded the impressions produced by his appearance at this period. "In the early part of July, 1856," he says, "I met him for the first time in Tibbie Shiel's Cottage. He had been making that charming spot—as rich in natural beauty as in associations with the best Scottish poetry and life of the last century—a residence for some days. He was then one of the masters of Rugby, and would be in his thirty-seventh year. I had come up Moffatdale, by Birkhill, and the Loch of the Lowes, through a day of sunshine, and by hillsides flecked with shadow, and it was now the 'gowden afternoon.' Passing through the gate which leads to the arbour of peace and quiet beauty, to me an oft-resting haunt, known as Tibbie Shiel's, the friend who was with me, pointing to the figure before the door, said, 'There is Shairp?' I had in my ear dim rumours of him, but had not met him before. A fair-haired, ruddy-faced,

and manly man—with open light gray-blue eyes—frank and
affable, with ready recognition. But what attracted me most
was that he was very wet—trousers, stockings, and boots
all fairly soaked. There was no waterproof trash of gearing
in those days; or, more probably, he despised it. He had
just come in from the upper hills, and had waded from one
glen to another, with a delightful sovereign contempt for the
plashing of the burns through which he had made his way.
This went to my heart at once. I was not generally at that
time inclined to respect a Rugby master. But, looking at
this Rugby master, in my soul I thought this must be a
good fellow, and he was. This was my first sight of, and
introduction to, Shairp; and, though I spoke but a few
words with him, I marked him inwardly as a congenial
and lovable man. How little can we judge of the inner
feeling of a man from outside appearance and casual
greeting! After that time—long after—I learned that he
was under the shadow of a family sorrow. Mrs Shairp
was with him, brought, I imagine, for the first time to
Yarrow,—a hope in him, I suppose, and well founded,
that she would share in its spirit—in the inner chord of
sympathy with the pathetic feeling of the place—perhaps
find some solace there."*

The visit here recorded gave rise to another poem,
characterised by an under-current of sadness. He had suffered
a sad bereavement, his son, " a more than commonly beautiful

---

* *Principal Shairp and His Friends,* by Professor Knight.

boy," having died. He found much solacement in this region
of "pastoral melancholy," for his grief-stricken heart, and he
has given expression to his feeling in one of the sweetest and
most touching poems he has ever written. During this
summer he was residing in Moffat, and later in the season, in
the month of August, he made another pilgrimage to ' Tibbie's,'
with Dean Stanley and Mr Godfrey Lushington as his
companions. It is this visit that he has commemorated in the
poem " Three Friends in Yarrow," which was not published
till after his death. All his poetry is informed by a pathetic
and tender spirit, and, as might be expected, these qualities
find their most perfect expression in his poems on Yarrow.

YARROW WATER.

It's not that the green hills are fair,
    And calm the lakes beneath them sleeping;
There's nothing there can e'er repair
    The sorrow we have long been weeping.

Though lambs are bleating far and near,
    And plaintive pipes the moorland plover,
A tenderer cry still haunts our ear,
    We shall no where on earth recover.

And yet if any place has felt
    The mellowing touch of human sorrow,
And into woeworn hearts could melt,
    Like healing balm, 'twere the braes of Yarrow.

o

There is a look o'er all these hills,
   A chastened look of tender meekness,
That feelingly o'er human ills
   Has brooded—mortal pain and weakness.

There lies St. Mary's tranced and lone,
   'Mid the old hills, their darling daughter, -
A song of the dim ages gone,
   Sings on for ever Yarrow Water.

And yet though gone the forest bield,
   The grey peel towers decaying slowly,
These hills have life that will not yield
   To fond regrets and sadness wholly.

They make the best of present boons,
   The golden lights, the summer weather,
And prank their slopes 'gainst autumn noons
   With streaks of bonny blooming heather.

And often at morning mist unfurled,
   At gloamin touched with spiritual feeling,
They seem to hint of that blest world
   Where weary hearts shall yet find healing.

NOTE.—This poem, which is here printed for the first time, was placed at my disposal by Mrs Shairp, who kindly consented, *at my urgent request*, to its publication.—R. B.

THREE FRIENDS IN YARROW.

O! many a year is gone, since in life's fresh dawn,
    The bonny forest over,
Morn to eve I wandered wide, as blithe as ever bride
    To meet her faithful lover.

From Newark's birchen bower, to Dryhope's hoary Tower,
    Peel and Keep I traced and numbered;
And sought o'er muir and brae, by cairn and cromlech grey,
    The graves where old warriors slumbered.

Where'er on hope or dale has lingered some faint trail
    Of song or minstrel glory,
There I drank deep draughts at will, but could never drink my
        fill,
    Of the ancient Border story.

O fond and foolish time, when to ballad and old rhyme
    Every throb of my pulse was beating!
As if old world things like these could minister heart-ease,
    Or the soul's deep want be meeting!

.   .   .   .

Now when gone is summer prime, and the mellow autumn
        time
    Of the year and of life has found us,
With thee, O gentle friend, how sweet one hour to spend,
    With the beauty of Yarrow all around us!

With him too for a guide, the Poet of Tweedside,
    Our steps 'mong the braes to order,
Who still doth prolong the fervour, torrent-strong,
    The old spirit of the Border.

Heaven's calm autumnal grey on holm and hillside lay,
    With here and there a gleaming ;
As the glints of sunny sheen down Herman's slopes of green
    O'er St. Mary's lake came dreaming.

There on Dryhope's Tower forlorn we marked the rowan, born
    From the rents of roofless ruin ;
And heard the [bridal] tale of the Flower of Yarrow Vale,
    And her old romantic wooing.

And then we wandered higher, where once St. Mary's quire
    O'er the still Lake watch was keeping :
But nothing now is seen save the lonely hillocks green,
    Where the Shepherds of Yarrow are sleeping.

And we stood by the stone where Piers Cockburn rests alone,
    With his Bride, in their dwelling narrow ;
And thou heard'st their tale of dool, and the wail of sorrow full,
    The saddest ever wailed on Yarrow.

Thou did'st listen, while thine eye all lovingly did lie
    On the green braes spread around thee ;
But I knew by the deep-rapt quiet thou did'st keep
    That the power of Yarrow had bound thee.

O, well that Yarrow should put on her sweetest mood
       To meet thy gentle being ;
For of both the native mien and the fortunes ye have seen,
       Respond with a strange agreeing.

There was beauty here before sorrow swept the Forest o'er,
       Its beauty more meek to render :—
Thou wert gentle from thy birth, and the toils and cares of
              earth
       Have but made thee more wisely tender.

High souls have come and gone, and on these braes have
              thrown
       The light of their glorious fancies,
And left their words to dwell and mingle with the spell
       Of a thousand old romances.

And who more fit to find [than] thou in soul and mind
       All akin to great bards departed,—
The high thoughts here they breathed, the boon they have
              bequeathed
       To all the tender hearted ?

And we who did partake, by still St. Mary's Lake,
       Those hours of renewed communion,
Shall feel, when far apart, the remembrance at our heart
       Keeps alive our foregone soul-union.

From this world of eye and ear soon we must disappear ;
       But our after-life may borrow
From these scenes some tone and hue, when all things are
              made new
       In a fairer land than Yarrow.

JOHN VEITCH.

———◆———

JOHN VEITCH was born at Peebles, October 24, 1829. He was educated in the Grammar School of his native town. At sixteen he matriculated as a student in Edinburgh University, where he had a highly distinguished career, more especially in logic and moral philosophy. Shortly after completing his course, the University conferred on him the degree of M.A., and some time after, that of LL.D. He was appointed to the chair of Logic and Rhetoric in St. Andrews in 1860, and to the same chair in Glasgow in 1864, a position which he still holds with much distinction.

In 1858 he wrote, by request of the Stewart trustees, the *Memoirs of Dugald Stewart.* He also acted as joint-editor, along with Dean Mansel, in superintending the publication of Sir William Hamilton's *Lectures on Metaphysics and Logic.* He has also translated the works of *Descartes.* In 1878 he published the *History and Poetry of the Scottish Border*, a work of great historical interest and value. This is the standard work on the subject, and will long hold a foremost place as a thoroughly safe and reliable guide book. Professor Veitch is an enthusiastic Borderer. Nowhere is he more at home than when wandering among the hills which environ the Tweed, the Manor, and the Yarrow. He is

familiar with every peak, and glen, and burn, between Tinto
and Minchmoor, and no one has given more perfect expression
to the weird, pathetic feeling which the natural scenery
of the district, combined with its tragic associations, creates
in the receptive mind and heart. Speaking of Professor
Veitch's poetry, a critic has remarked :—" Next to an autumn
day among the hills themselves, commend us to poems like
these, in which so much of the finer breath and spirit of those
pathetic hills is distilled into melody." Professor Veitch's
principal poetical works are *Hillside Rhymes*, published 1872 ;
The Tweed and other Poems, 1875 ; *Merlin*, 1889.

IN YARROW.

JANUARY 2, 1886.

I'll see Newhall this winter day,
 The withered hills to me are dear ;
The lint-white bent, the bracken brown,
 Ye well beseem the faded year.

And restful all the heights around,
 Their greenery spent, the summer gone,
Now waiting in a blissful calm,
 With quiet faith, the April sun.

Nor without omen now of hope,—
 The sky-blue rift, the sunny gleam,
The soft wind bearing light and shade,
 The leaping voices of the stream.

I muse and pass by lone Glenlude,
   There Yarrow spreads before my sight,
The grey clouds moving part, and throw
   O'er the brown hills a dappled light.

No gliding stream art thou, this morn,
   Thy flood each branching channel fills;
In gleaming spears adown the vale
   Thou pours't three Yarrows from the hills :

In roaring sweep of Border fray,
   Thou risest in this year new born ;
Untouched by age, untamed by time,
   In strength as of thy earliest morn.

Now flow with all thy torrent force,
   Bring pulsing of thy mighty heart,
Then softly voice the mournful strain,
   Heard when fate-stricken lovers part.

Whate'er the years to come may hold,
   Of love or power or tragic deed,
Well canst thou match the wondrous tale,
   Let maiden sigh or warrior bleed.

Beseems the well the gentle tide
   That flows in summer's gloamin' time;
Befits thee well the forceful mood
   'Neath this grey sky and winter clime.

Thou'st known the craving heart of love,
　The hapless fate of dule and sorrow,
The yearning for the south wind's breath
　To waft a kiss to her on Yarrow.

Thou'st known the manly form outstretched
　Face upwards on the benty heath,
No braver man than he laid low,
　Nor stronger arm now limp in death.

Thou hast so framed our souls to these,
　Well may'st thou leap and flash to-day ;
No grander man, no nobler maid
　Shall live than in thy Ballad lay.

ST. MARY'S LOCH.

From Rodono, Evening of September 5, 1884.

Thou canst not stay, dear Loch, unmoved beneath
This moon, the full-orbed eager eye that glows
Above thy southern hills, and holds thee bound
By passionate face of olden memories ;
Under the beam thou racest from the east,
In long drawn ripples, bright from shore to shore,
Thy deep full heart leaps up in joyous mood,
Free-bound in moving links of silver sheen,

The eager unconstraint of new-born love.
O'er thee thy guardian hills bend gleaming, fused,
Faint-dimmed, in the transparent veil, where now
In middle-air the olden visions float,—
The love-lorn maiden of the Forest Kirk,
Her face whose tears bedewed the Dowie Den,
The lovers fleeing o'er the moonlit bent,
The widow wailing sore her loved-slain lord,—
The dead that know not death,—assembled there
Serene and still, as is the pearly cloud
Of this night's heaven, whose calm encircles thee,
　　Thou gentle, conquering moon!

THE DOW GLEN:

In the Henderland Burn.

———

Soft downwards glides the burnie
　　Into its deep dark Linn;
The rude grey rocks encircling,
　　Listen the quiet din.

Two rowans twine their branches,
　　Where streamlet fills its urn;
And gleam and shade are flecking
　　The waters as they turn.

On this fair morn of summer,
  When the green is on the hill,
And every glen keeps silence
  For the music of its rill ;

No marvel, Linn, old-storied,
  Thou sharest the heart spread wide,
In sunny sheen arraying
  Thy gentle lapsing tide.

As if thou'dst know no sorrow,
  Ne'er heard a woman's wail,
And only note of gladness
  Been wafted down thy Vale.

Yet once no deeper outburst
  Heard the ages in their course,
Nor passion thrown to heaven,
  In fiercer torrent force ;

As from the wife heart-broken,
  Thy waters bore the cry,
And the forest hills in echo
  Woke the world's sympathy.

Ah, me ! she hears the shouting,
  Where she cowers beside the Linn ;
Around her lord men crowding,
  And all the dying din.

A stroke of death, none feller
   Hath ever flashed from cloud ;
In joy of life at morning,
   At eve low in his blood.

And none now knows her story,
   Where human heart doth dwell,
But weeps the woman watching
   The dead she loved so well ;

But weeps the widow " happing "
   Alone the form clay-cold,
In tender consecration
   To the keeping of the mould.

Linn ! in mine ear thy cadence
   Hath its own peculiar fall ;
As echo of a sorrow,
   Through time which softens all.

And thy bright lapse, short-gleaming,
   Of a life the symbol meet,
Whose joy all sudden closes,
   As in dark pool at thy feet.

Clings to thy rock thy ivy,
   To keep faith's memory green ;
And the red rose of the briar
   Glows where her love hath been,

A love that is undying,
    As thou, Linn, goest ever on,
In rise and fall aye soughing
    In sorrow's monotone.

IN MEMORIAM:

Rev. JAMES RUSSELL, D.D., Yarrow.

———

A morn of mist and weeping rain,
    As well befits our sorrow,
Hangs o'er thy vale, and o'er thy stream,
    Thou grievest—rueful Yarrow!

The courtly grace, the kindly face,
    Thou keepest not his marrow,
A quiet, self-sufficing life
    He lived by thee, O Yarrow!

Of restless aim or fickle fame,
    No comfort would he borrow,
But he would live the people's friend,
    And be thy lover, Yarrow!

By deed of blood, by hopeless love,
    Thou every heart canst harrow,
Thy spirit in our gentle friend
    Was purified, O Yarrow!

The strife of life he heeded not,
　　His joy to heal the sorrow
That fell upon each humble heart,
　　By thy clear wave, O Yarrow!

On every hill, in every glen,
　　To meet him was good morrow,
Now blithesome lark may o'er him trill
　　On thy dowie houms, O Yarrow!

I've seen thee oft at winter tide,
　　But ne'er so sad beforrow,
Ne'er fern so seer, nor bent so wan,
　　Nor birk so bare in Yarrow!

The pastor and the friend is gone,
　　Be his a brighter morrow
Than ever dawned upon the vale,
　　Even thine! O winsome Yarrow!

IN MEMORIAM:

THE REV. THOMAS M'CRINDLE, FOR 39 YEARS MINISTER OF THE FREE CHURCH IN THE PARISH OF YARROW.

———

No conquering hero come we here to crown,
Or round a scholar's brow the wreathe entwine;
His gentle sway of pure and simple heart,
And noble lesson of the life divine.

One Master his, and Him to serve alone —
All heedless of the world, its bribe or blame,
A lowly life 'mid atmosphere of heaven
He lived, well worthy of the Christ-like name.
Ah! gentle soul! once Yarrow knew coarse times,
Dispeace and strife and voices bold and rude,
'Twas yours to touch us with a finer strain,
The loving peace of Christian brotherhood.

JAMES BROWN.

———◆———

JAMES BROWN, better known
in the literary world as "J. B.
Selkirk," was born at Selkirk in
the year 1832. He received his
early training in one of the schools
of his native town, at that time
famous throughout the Borders as
an educational centre, and sub-
sequently was sent to The
Institution in Edinburgh,

where he completed his education. He has been from an early period of life a frequent contributor to Magazine literature—*Blackwood* and *Cornhill* especially having been favoured with numerous contributions, in prose and verse, from his prolific pen. He is also the author of the following works:—*Bible Truths and Shakespearian Parallels* (Longman's, 1862), published in four editions since; *Poems* (Longman's, 1869); *Ethics and Æsthetics of Modern Poetry* (Smith, Elder & Co., 1878); *Yarrow and other Poems* (Kegan Paul, Trench & Co., 1883). These works display literary qualities of a high order. His poems on Yarrow are full of local colouring. No poet has ever sung the praises of the classic Vale who knew it more intimately, and few indeed have so perfectly caught the spirit of the place, or given to it such an exquisite literary expression. "J. B. Selkirk's" poems on Yarrow will be read and admired as long as the district possesses charms for the poetic mind.

A SONG OF YARROW.

September, and the sun was low,
   The tender greens were flecked with yellow,
And autumn's ardent after-glow
   Made Yarrow's uplands rich and mellow.

P

Between me and the sunken sun,
  Where gloaming gathered in the meadows,
Contented cattle, red and dun,
  Were slowly browsing in the shadows.

And out beyond them Newark reared
  Its quiet tower against the sky,
As if its walls had never heard
  Of wassail-rout or battle cry.

O'er moss-grown roofs that once had rung,
  To reiver's riot, Border brawl,
The slumberous shadows mutely hung,
  And silence deepened over all.

Above the high horizon bar
  A cloud of golden mist was lying,
And over it a single star
  Soared heavenward as the day was dying.

No sound, no word, from field or ford,
  Nor breath of wind to float a feather,
While Yarrow's murmuring waters poured
  A lonely music through the heather.

In silent fascination bound,
  As if some mighty spell obeying,
The hills stood listening to the sound,
  And wondering what the stream was saying.

What secret to the inner ear,
  What happier message was it bringing,
With more of hope, and less of fear,
  Than men dare mix with earthly singing?

Earth's song it was, yet heavenly growth—
  It was not joy, it was not sorrow—
A strange heart-fulness of them both,
  The wandering singer seemed to borrow.

Like one that sings and does not know,
  But in a dream hears voices calling,
Of those that died long years ago,
  And sings although the tears be falling.

Oh Yarrow! garlanded with rhyme
  That clothes thee in a mournful glory,
Though sunsets of an elder time
  Had never crowned thee with a story,—

Still would I wander by thy stream,
  Still listen to the lonely singing,
That gives me back the golden dream
  Through which old echoes yet are ringing.

Love's sunshine! sorrow's bitter blast!
  Dear Yarrow, we have seen together;
For years have come, and years have past
  Since first we met among the heather.

Ah! those, indeed, were happy hours
   When first I knew thee, gentle river;
But now thy bonny birken bowers
   To me, alas, are changed for ever!

The best, the dearest, all have gone,
   Gone like the bloom upon the heather,
And left us singing here alone,
   Beside life's cold and winter weather.

I, too, pass on, but when I'm dead,
   Thou still shalt sing by night and morrow,
And help the aching heart and head
   To bear the burden of its sorrow.

And summer flowers shall linger yet
   Where all thy mossy margins guide thee;
And minstrels, met as we have met,
   Shall sit and sing their songs beside thee.

DEATH IN YARROW.

I.

It's no the sax month gane,
   Sin' a' our cares began—
Sin' she left us here alane,
   Her callant and gudeman.
It was in the Spring she dee'd,
   And now we're in the fa';
And sair we've struggled wi't,
   Sin' his mother gaed awa'.

II.

An awfu' blow was that—
   The deed that nane can dree;
And lang and sair we grat
   For her we couldna see.
I've aye been strong and fell,
   And can stand a gey bit thraw;
But the laddie's no hissel'
   Sin' his mother gaed awa'.

III.

In a' the water-gate,
   Ye couldna find his marrow—
There wasna' ane his mate,
   In Ettrick Shaws or Yarrow.
But he hasna now the look
   He used to hae ava;
He's grown sae little buik
   Sin' his mother gaed awa'.

IV.

I tak' him on my back,
   In ilka blink o' sun,
Rin roun' about the stack,
   And mak'-believe its fun.
But weel he kens, I warrant,
   There's something wrang for a',
He's turned sae auld farrant
   Sin' his mother gaed awa'.

v.

For when he's play'd his fill,
 I canna help but see,
How he draws the creepie stool
 Aye the closer to my knee;
And he turns his muckle een
 To the picter on the wa',
Wi' a face grown thin and keen,
 Sin' his mother gaed awa'.

vi.

I mak' his pickle meat—
 And I think I mak' it weel;
And I warm his little feet,
 When I hap him i' the creel;
And he kisses me fu' couthie,
 For he downa' sleep at a'
Till he hauds up his bit mouthie,
 Sin' his mother gaed awa'.

vii.

And then I dander oot
 When I can do nae mair,
And walk the hills aboot,
 I dinna aye ken where;
For my hairt's wi' ane abune,
 And the ane is growin' twa,
He's dwined sae sair, sae sune,
 Sin' his mother gaed awa.

VIII.

And now the lang day's dune,
    And the nicht's begun to fa',
And a bonnie harvest mune
    Rises up on Bowerhope Law.
It's a bonnie warlt this,
    But it's no' for me at a',
For a' thing's gane amiss
    Sin' his mother gaed awa'.

RETREAT IN YARROW:

Dobb's Linn.

In the green bosom of the sunny hills,
Far from the weary sound of human ills,
    Where silence sleepeth,
Where nothing breaks the still and charmèd hours
Save whispering mountain stream that 'neath the flowers
    For ever creepeth.

In the green bosom of the sunny hills
There let me live : where dewy freshness fills
    The stainless sky,—
Where, out of very love, the mighty breeze
That wildly wanders over heaving seas
    Lies down to die.

There let me live, there let me watch on high
Wild winter send adown the stormy sky
        His howling crew.
Or when from heaven in the perfect time
Great summer sheddeth in her rosy prime
        Joy-tears of dew.

My teachers are the hills; no truth that feigns
A subtle wisdom drawn from weary brains
        With laboured care,
But nature's teaching, that from daisied sod
To lark-sung heights can find the love of God
        Plain written everywhere.

My God is in the hills; and men have left
Earth's temples, when of house and home bereft,
        In truth's despair,
To seek among the hills, in hunted bands,
God's higher temple never built with hands,
        And found it there.

Oh silent Hills, Oh everlasting Hills!
Whether the summer clothes or winter chills
        Thy holy brow!
Worshipping God for ever, while the breath
Of man dies out on meat that perisheth,
        How beautiful art thou!

The restless fevered wave of human life
Is echoing down the ages, but the strife
   Disturbs not thee.
Oh, mountain! sending up thy ceaseless prayer,
Fervently silent, through the charmèd air
   Of heaven's blue sea.

The birth, the glory, or the fall of nations,
Is naught to thee ! delirious generations,
   Ceasing never !
Rave onward, and thou heedest not the chase,
But lookest up serenely in the face
   Of God for ever !

ANDREW LANG.

———◆———

ANDREW LANG was born at Selkirk on the 31st of March, 1844. He was educated at the Edinburgh Academy, St. Andrew's University, and Balliol College, Oxford. He is an M.A. and LL.D. In 1868 he was elected a Fellow of Merton College, Oxford. His contributions to literature are numerous. The following are among his principal works:—*Ballades in Blue China* (1881), *Helen of Troy* (1882), *Rhymes a la mode* (1884), *Custom and Myth* (1884), &c., &c., &c.

He was appointed by the Senatus of St. Andrew's University to deliver a course of lectures on Natural Theology, under the Gifford Trust, and it is expected that these will shortly be given to the world in book form. He writes in the *Daily News* and *St. James's Gazette*, and several of his recent publications have been reprinted from these sources. His contributions to periodical literature are numerous. Indeed, there are few Scotsmen more widely known or highly esteemed in the literary world.

A SUNSET IN YARROW.

The wind and the day had lived together,
    They died together, and far away
Spoke farewell in the sultry weather,
One of the sunset, over the heather,
    The dying wind and the dying day.
Far in the south, the summer even'
    Flushed a flame in the grey soft air,
We seemed to look on the hills of heaven
You saw within, but to me 'twas given
    To see your face, as an angel's, there.
Never again, ah! surely never
    Shall we wait and watch as of old we stood,
The low good night of the hill and the river,
The faint light fade, and the wan stars quiver,
    Twain grown one in the solitude.

ALEXANDER ANDERSON.

———————◆———————

ALEXANDER ANDERSON was born at Kirkconnel, Dumfriesshire, on the 30th April, 1845. He was educated at the village school of Crocketford, Galloway, to which place his parents had removed when he was quite young. In course of time he returned to his native place, and for a considerable number of years was engaged on the railway as a surfacemen. An occupation of this nature is by no means favourable to mental culture, or the development of poetical tastes; but genius, in the long run, is sure to assert itself, however unfavourable the environment. While engaged in this way he acquired a knowledge of French, German, and Italian, in order, as he says, that he might be able to " appreciate, in their own tongue, the mighty voices of Goethe, Schiller, and Dante." A poem on John Keats, published in the *People's Friend*, at once brought him into notice. His *Song of Labour and other Poems* was published in 1873, and at once met with a most generous reception from the press and the public. *The Two Angels and other Poems* (1875); *Songs of the Rail* (1878); *Ballads and Sonnets* (1879).

His subsequent contributions to poetical literature have amply fulfilled the promise of his first efforts. For some years Mr Anderson has acted as one of the librarians in the University of Edinburgh—a situation thoroughly congenial to his tastes.

Long before he visited the district, he manifested a lively interest in the literature and romance of Yarrow. His first impressions of the Vale are finely expressed in the poem "In Yarrow." It will there be seen how thoroughly he was in touch with its soul-stirring traditions. Though one of the latest, he is certainly not one of the least of those around whom Yarrow has thrown the mantle of her inspiration.

IN YARROW.

A dream of youth has grown to fruit.
    Though years it was in blossom ;
It lay, like touch of summer light,
    Far down within my bosom :
It led me on from hope to hope,
    Made rainbows of each morrow,
And now my heart has had its wish—
    I stood to-day in Yarrow.

And as I stood, my old sweet dreams
    Took back their long-lost brightness;
My boyhood came, and in my heart
    Rose up a summer lightness;

I heard faint echoes of far song
   Grow rich and deep, and borrow
The low, sweet tones of early years—
   I stood to-day in Yarrow.

O dreams of youth, dreamt long ago,
   When every hour was pleasure !
O hopes that come when Hope was high,
   Nor niggard of her treasure !—
Ye come to-day, and, as of old,
   I could not find your marrow ;
Ye made my heart grow warm with tears—
   I stood to-day in Yarrow.

That touch of sorrow when our youth
   Was in its phase of sadness,
For which no speech was on the lip,
   To frame its gentle madness,
Rests on each hill I saw to-day,
   Till I was left with only
That pleasure which is almost pain,
   The sense of being lonely.

The haunting sense of love, that now
   Beats with a feebler pinion,
Above the shatter'd domes that once
   Soared high in his dominion ;
And in the air of all that time,
   Nor joy nor sadness wholly,
Seem all to mix and melt away
   In pleasing melancholy.

Why should it be that, as we dream,
　A tender song of passion,
Of lovers loving long ago,
　In the old Border fashion,
Should touch and hallow every spot,
　Until its presence thorough
Is in the very grass that throbs
　With thoughts of love and Yarrow.

We know not; we can only deem
　The heart lives in the story,
And gives to stream and hill around
　A lover's tearful glory,
Until it bears us back to feel,
　The light of that far morrow
That touch'd the ridge on Tinnis Hill,
　Then fell on winding Yarrow.

Ah, not on Yarrow stream alone
　Fell that most tender feeling,
But like a light from out a light,
　An inmost charm revealing,
It lay, and lies on vale and hill,
　On waters in their flowing;
And only can the heart discern
　The source of its bestowing.

Yes! we may walk by Yarrow stream
　With speech, and song, and laughter,
But still far down a sadness sleeps,
　To wake and follow after.

And soft regrets that come and go,
   The light and shade of sorrow,
Are with me still, that I may know
   I stood to-day in Yarrow.

ON YARROW BRAES.

The wind, the summer wind of June,
   Was on our cheeks as, in the heather,
We lay that happy afternoon
   On Yarrow braes together.

Far down below was Yarrow Manse,
   Within its little woodland hiding,
And by it, like a silver glance,
   The stream itself was gliding.

And farther up in greyer light,
  The " dowie dens " lay in their shadow,
And only half made out to sight
  By spots of corn and meadow.

And Tinnis hill rose huge and steep,
  Its ridge against the sky receding ;
And white upon its breast the sheep
  By twos and threes were feeding.

Westward from Yarrow Kirk, within,
  A field that speaks of love and loving,
A single stone was seen to win
  The eye from all its roving.

Ah ! well it might, for round that stone
  Such tender consecration hovers,
That love might rest his cheek thereon
  And weep for hopeless lovers.

And in the wind that came and went,
  We heard a music weird and lonely ;
The past was in its tones and blent
  With human sorrow only.

And pity for all things that love
  Has set in legendary story
To haunt grey crag and hill, and move
  Round ruins bleak and hoary.

Q

The dim old world of song that sings
  Of tender love in old romances,
Was with us, touching all the strings
  That woke our saddest fancies.

We heard the sounds of wail and pain,
  Faint from that far-off time of sorrow ;
The misty years came back again,
  And look'd with us on Yarrow.

All this, and more, that summer day,
  Was with us, as among the heather,
A ballad on our lips, we lay
  On Yarrow braes together.

ST. MARY'S LAKE.

Away from all the restless street,
  The whirlpool of the toiling race,
Where traffic in the dusty heat,
  Toils with the sweat upon his face.

Away from these, and far away,
  We fight the strong wind on the hill,
Or rest upon the bracken'd brae,
  And shape our dreamland as we will.

What boon to lie, as now I lie,
  And see in silver at my feet
Saint Mary's Lake, as if the sky
  Had fallen 'tween those hills so sweet,

And this old churchyard on the hill,
   That keeps the green graves of the dead,
So calm and sweet, so lone and still,
   And but the blue sky overhead.

Ah ! here they lie, the simple race,
   Who lived their little flight of years,
Then laid them in this quiet place,
   At rest for ever from their fears.

The winds sing as they sang to them,
   The bracken changes as of old,
The hills still wear their diadem
   Of heather, and the sunset's gold.

No change in these ; the waves still break
   In ripple or in foam upon
The green shores of Saint Mary's lake,
   As in the ages dead and gone.

Beneath the hills where shadows seem
   Fit haunts for lonely sounds that be,
Flows, half in sunshine, Yarrow stream,
   Th' spirit of all I hear and see.

Thou Yarrow of my early dreams,
   When fancy heard thee murmur on,
A light has pass'd from other streams,
   And deepens all thy haunting tone.

It crowns thee with a magic dower ;
  It makes thy windings ever sweet ;
The Mary Scott of Dryhope Tower,
  Still follows thee with unseen feet.

Her name is wed to thine ; the vale
  Is witness as thou rollest on,
And with thee all the tender wail
  Of song, with sorrow in its tone.

Men pass from thee ; the years prolong,
  No name of theirs for ear or eye ;
But she—a little whirl of song
  Has caught her, and she cannot die,

And lying on the bracken'd hill,
  The sunshine on my brow to-day,
The old love-ballad echoes still,
  In throbs that will not pass away.

And as I listen, like a dream
  That changes into softer things,
Saint Mary's Lake and Yarrow stream
  Take all the sorrow which it sings.

YARROW STREAM.

From Selkirk unto Newark Tower,
We walk'd beneath the gentle power
Of old-world song, that chants and sings
Amid the rush of modern things,

And all our thoughts that came and went,
And lightly with each fancy blent,
Had for refrain to wander through
Some snatch of ballad song, that drew
Its inspiration from the gleam,
The sweep, and glide of Yarrow stream.

Oh ! sweet in Harewood sang the birds,
The sound of summer in their chords :
They sang as only birds can sing
When sunshine ripples throat and wing,
And through each opening of the trees
Made by the fingers of the breeze,
We saw in circles far below,
Like silver in the western glow,
The spirit of our evening dream,
Whose murmurs came from Yarrow stream.

And Carterhaugh was in our sight,
On which a legend rests like light ;
Bowhill against its height was seen,
Half-hid amid its wealth of green ;
And every spot would waft along
Some fragment of an early song,
Sung when the heart was fresh, and drew
Its melody as heath the dew,
And over all the tender beam
Of fading light on Yarrrow stream.

Oh ! here should be a perfect home,
For love and lovers when they come,
With whispered words and gentle sighs,
To draw a sweet delight from eyes,
Nor care for any other speech
But tender looks to answer each ;
And hand in hand to stray, and deem
Their spirits one with Yarrow stream.

The sigh of winds and song of birds,
The whispered tones of lovers' words—
These should be all that Yarrow heard
Since first its lonely source was stirred.
Alas ! far other music rang
When Border knights to saddle sprang,
When over all the bugle blew
A note each winding valley knew,
When strong of arm they sternly led,
With mail on breast and helm on head,
The foray in the light of day,
Or with the moon to show the way,

Woke the strange echoes of the night,
With sudden shouts of party fight.
Ah, what to them was each sweet beam
Of silver light on Yarrow stream !

On Philiphaugh the grass is green
As if no battle there had been,
The flowers bloom without that hue
Their ruddier sisters felt and knew,
That morn when other drops than rain
Fell with a touch that left a stain ;
The lark still sings the self-same lay
His earlier brothers sang that day,
When all the jar of battle smote
And drown'd the gushing of each note.
The winds are still as fresh and sweet,
The grass as green beneath our feet,
The mavis in his solitude
Sends prayers of music through the wood,
The sunsets die in golden gleam,
And Yarrow still is Yarrow stream.

No change for Yarrow, save that change
That comes with seasons as they range.
No change, though Newark's rugged form
That still gives battle to the storm
Should slowly crumble down, and pass
Nor leave one trace of where it was,
Save in the melody of two
Who turn'd them to the past, and drew

Such inspiration that around
Their brows the singing wreaths were bound.
And now in that high atmosphere
The winds of death make sweet and clear,
They shine apart from any wrong,
The sun and moon of Border song.
No change, for Yarrow still will glide,
The same sweet music in its tide,
The merle still pipe in Hangingshaw,
The lark sing over Carterhaugh ;
And sweet St. Mary's Lake between
The hills, still show her silver sheen,
As if to know were joy to her
That Yarrow was her worshipper.
For drawing from her waves so lone
The liquid pulses of its own,
Whose beats make music full and strong,
Till Ettrick mingles with the song.

All these remain ; but we who gaze,
After our little term of days,
Shall pass to claim, as right of birth,
Our little freehold from the earth,
On which a thousand springs that pass
In pity shall renew the grass.
Then Yarrow, as it glides away
By meadow, hill, and glen to-day,
Shall be the same to those who hear
Its haunting murmurs in their ear ;
And other hearts than ours shall deem
That Yarrow still is Yarrow stream.

ST MARY'S LOCH: A REMINISCENCE, 1856.

THE following poem, by an anonymous author, has been kindly placed at my disposal by Professor Knight, St. Andrews. It gives expression to a feeling which many who have visited St. Mary's Loch will be able heartily to appreciate. Only now and again is the water perfectly placid, reflecting in its silent depths the features of the surrounding country. The swan may be seen any day, but not always the shadow.

> The breeze comes gently from the west,
>   The lake is gleaming brightly,
> From smiling ripple to the crest
>   Of wavelet dancing lightly.
>
> No quiet rest, no mirrored hills,
>   In placid apparition,
> No steadfast azure which fulfils
>   Its own sweet repitition.
>
> Fast float the cloudlets through the sky,
>   Fast fly the shadows under;
> Gone is the fair serenity
>   That moved our fancy's wonder.

Yet rest we not, for mirrored still,
　　In every changing feature,
The earth, in lake, and sky, and hill,
　　Reflects our human nature.

The freshening lake, the brightening skies,
　　—Half-veiling, half-revealing—
Reflect they not in mystic guise
　　The fulness of our feeling ?

And thoughts within are lightly stirred
　　By every floweret blowing,
By moorland sound, by glancing bird,
　　By gentle rillets flowing.

We take great Nature to our heart,
　　And every passing minute,
She soothes us with a sweet unrest,
　　That has no sorrow in it.

Thus bear we with us wandering on,
　　By meadow or by river,
A beauty that our hearts have won,
　　And shall possess for ever.

A REMEMBRANCE OF YARROW,

BY

CONSTANCE W. MANGIN, born 1856.

The sun shone warm from its noonday height,
Bathing the valley in mellow light,
While far below like a silver thread,
The river rolled o'er its rocky bed.

How oft from those dreamy slopes ere now,
The heathy breeze had swept my brow;
Recalling dreams and memories fond,
And thoughts of peace from the land beyond.

How well I know each billowy form,
In sunlight or shadow, calm or storm;
One moment still as a sleeping child,
Then dark and murk as the ocean wild.

Yarrow! where lies the fascination,
Binding heart and imagination;
Thrilling the pulses of those that dwell
Beneath the charm of thy mystic spell!

Is it thy scars so rugged and bold?
Or thy countless hills together rolled?
Or thy misty slopes and dowie dens,
And lovers' trysts in the birchen glens?

Or thy murmuring burns, which softly glide
Through caves where the brown trout love to hide ?
The shadowy pool, where fern and heath
A fairy bower have twined beneath ?

The distant swoop of the curlew's flight,
A moment passing, then lost to sight ;
Winging her way to her grassy nest,
Concealed in some rugged moss-grown crest ?

    .   .   .   .

Long years have passed, and the Yarrow stream
Remains to me but a sunny dream
Of joy and youth and love together,
And children's steps among the heather.

E'en now, as I watch the embers glow,
I hear its gurgling eddying flow,
And see it wander through the mead,
Losing itself in silvery Tweed.

ANNIE S. SWAN.

A NNIE S. SWAN was born at Leith in the year 1859. She began her literary career at an early period of life, and has attained great popularity as a writer of fiction. Many of her books have gone through several editions. The following are a few of her best known works:—*Aldersyde*— the scene of which is laid in Yarrow,—*Carlowrie ; The Gates of Eden ; Divided Hearts ; Sheila ;* &c., &c., &c.

ST. MARY'S.

In deep and mystic loveliness, engirt
By an unbroken boundlessness of rest,
With rocky steep and shadowy mountain peak,
  Clear mirrored on the silver of thy breast.
Oh, loved and lone St. Mary's! Thou indeed
Art rich in solemn sad sweet memories!
Each gentle winding of thy waters deep
Seems charged with wealth of by-gone mystery.
Dear haunt of many a noble heart and true,
There lingers still about thy wave-kissed shore
A halo of the past. A something thrills
Like spoken word of those that are no more,
Though many a bard has tuned his lyre for thee,
Accept this mite of gratitude from me.

THOMAS RAE.

THOMAS RAE, born at Galashiels, 19th October, 1868;
died 11th Sept., 1889.

YARROW.
(A MEMORY).

'Tis but an old time dream which comes
  Before my fading gaze,
Of rugged mountain, lake, and fell,
  Flitting through memory's haze.

A joy long past : but, now, the dream
  Born out of childhood's years,
Comes softly, full of tenderness,
  Amidst my falling tears.

'Twas when a boy, I wandered lone,
  Beside its banks so narrow,
And listened to its mournful dirge—
  The spirit of the Yarrow.

Ev'n then I felt its mystic power,
  Nor knew not why't should daunt me,
And, now, tho' years have come and gone,
  These old-time feelings haunt me.

I fain would seek thy solitude,
  And tread thy banks once more ;
To hear the murmur of thy song,
  Dear to this heart of yore.

I know that thou art still the same,
    Yet changèd, too, thou'lt be,
Since the old hearts of that sweet time
    Are dead, and gone from me !

Yet thou, O hallowed mystic spot,
    Their slumb'ring dust art keeping,
And in thy churchyard, silent, lone,
    These old hearts low are sleeping.

And so I ever dream of thee,
    With joy akin to sorrow ;
Thou'rt dear to me for what has been,
    Lonely and silent Yarrow !